COUNSELLING AND THERAPY

COUNSELLING AND THERAPY
The Spiritual Dimension

PIR VILAYAT INAYAT KHAN

A CONDOR BOOK
SOUVENIR PRESS (E&A) LTD

Copyright © by Omega Publications

First published in the USA by
Omega Publications, New Lebanon
under the title *Introducing Spirituality into
Counseling and Therapy*

First British edition published 1993 by
Souvenir Press (Educational & Academic) Ltd,
43 Great Russell Street, London WC1B 3PA

ISBN 0 285 63161 6

Printed in Great Britain by
The Guernsey Press Co. Ltd, Guernsey, Channel Islands

The author is indebted to Sajjada Kopelman, who assembled the transcribed lectures on which this book is based, and to Alison Kilgour, who skillfully transformed the spoken word into written style.

CONTENTS

COUNSELLING AND THERAPY

Chapter 1:

NEW SETTINGS OF CONSCIOUSNESS

To understand the spiritual dimensions of counseling, the first thing we must be prepared to do is to reverse our way of looking at things. Instead of thinking of ourselves as the witness who is trying to sort out another person's problems, we must imagine ourselves as being thought of by God. This reversal of the normal self-image of the counselor is, in fact, the Sufi point of view: that it is always God who is the knower, the thinker, the feeler, or the witness, while we are simply the media through which the knowing, the thinking, the feeling, and the witnessing take place. Normally, we are caught in our personal vantage point, and from that vantage point we cannot understand things clearly; so the premise on which our whole work can be based is the necessity for reaching out beyond the limits of our personal vantage point into a wider consciousness.

We must all face the fact that we are very precariously suspended in life: we have a very slender foothold on the planet. There is a certain insecurity in the unconscious mind that is due to its awareness of the transience of the human being. In moments of despair, the fear of extinction—of having to meet death—is involved, although we may not always care to admit it. Even more serious for many people is the fear of failure—of not even "making good" the short period of time allotted them. Human beings who identify themselves with all those aspects of their beings that are transient are desperately fighting extinction and failure in their search for meaningfulness.

Parallel to this point of view, however, is a transcendent awareness that can never be explained by the mind or constricted by the personal vantage point: the sense of eternity and infinity. Our problem is how to reconcile the saving grace of transcendent awareness—the safety buoy in our lives—with the personal vantage point. The only way to do this is to defy the laws of syllogistic logic in which we have been brought up.

In the realm of science, and particularly in physics, it has become very clear that something has to give in our way of understanding things. At the moment, that something is syllogistic logic—the tendency of the mind to compartmentalize things into categories. Now we find that we must accept the reality of contradictory truths.

The fact that the human being is both eternal and transient at the same time is an example of a contradictory truth. The syllogism, "Man is mortal; Socrates is a man; therefore Socrates is mortal," is setting up categories. What we must do to overcome this logic is to have the experience of eternity or infinity. In fact, we do experience eternity and infinity continually, but we tend to eliminate this experience from our *imago mundi*—our picture of the world—when we focus on our personal consciousness.

To understand what happens to the human being in our ordinary state of awareness, which is the vantage point of the person, we can use the functioning of the eyes as a metaphor. Our eyes are essentially lenses: they reduce the panorama to an image so that the totality of the experience of the physical world is reduced by the lenses of the eyes. But because we have two eyes, there are two images, and the brain is able to integrate the information from those two images and construct from them an approximation of the physical perspective. By using two eyes, we have a hologram-like way of experiencing things instead of a purely lens-like way: the two images are decoded by the brain to produce a three-dimensional picture, which is a reduced representation of reality that is, at least, richer than the picture formed by only one eye.

Consciousness functioning in human beings, as well as in other forms of life, is also a combination of lens-like and hologram-like functioning: we alternate between the two, so that we might say that universal, or hologram-like, consciousness is focalized in what we call "my consciousness" or "your consciousness" when we see things from a focalized, lens-like angle, which is the personal vantage point. At the moment when our consciousness is offset from its lens-like functioning, there is an oceanic feeling of being the total reality. When the personal self has been totally obliterated, there is an awareness of what one really is. Once again defying logic, we learn that we are not only transient and eternal at the same time, but also both part of the totality and the totality at the same time.

This point of view is challenging to orthodox ideology, yet this is what we experience at those rare moments called "peak experiences" by Abraham Maslow. Maslow divides human beings (if we may permit him to categorize) into "peakers" and "nonpeakers," and notes that "peakers" often find it hard to convey to "nonpeakers" how things look when one peaks. In spite of this, we know that there is an ineffable aura of experience beyond our concrete, focalized experience. This experience is unaccountable; it does not fit into any of the categories of our minds, and some people have a great deal of difficulty in dealing with it because when consciousness is oscillated into those areas beyond the personal consciousness, the experience seems very much like simple reverie, and they find themselves less able to function in time and space. People who are in a very high state of consciousness because their consciousness is not limited by a strong ego sense sometimes find it difficult to function in time and space.

An athlete running a race tends to be very conscious of time and space: he or she is in the here and now. The mystic, of course, is in the everywhere and always, less centered in his or her self-awareness. Nature has made human beings in such a way as to equip us with the ability to survive physically, and consequently the whole framework of our being is a compromise. Human beings normally function within the middle ranges of the universe. At short distances, two parallel lines never meet, but at long distances they do; the human being is made to function in the realm where two parallel lines never meet—a middle range that is superbly adapted to supermarket shopping or crossing the street, but which gives no understanding of meaningfulness. Since the greatest use of our lives involves more than space-time relationships, we must learn to modify consciousness at will in order to get into the wider settings of consciousness.

Thus far we have looked at the problem from the standpoint of the person—the individual—but since that is precisely where our limitation lies, we should rather look at the individual from the overall point of view: instead of expanding consciousness in the vastness of the cosmos, we should experience the divine consciousness crowded into the personal focus. This is the whole miracle of life as expressed by Prentice Mulford when he wrote, "We want nothing but the impossible possibility," which he described as "Infinity in a finite fact and eternity in a temporal act."

This is the secret of life and the very basis of Christianity: that perfection should be present in imperfection, that the divine perfection should come through in a body that is mortal—or at the very least be subject to the nature of bodiness, even though it is continually challenging that constriction, which in Judaism is called *tzum-tzum.* We now have scientific confirmation of what has been believed from the beginning of time by the Hindus: that every fraction of the totality contains the totality in it, at least implicitly or potentially. Scientists have learned that every cell of the body contains the genetic code of the whole body, which means that every part of the body contains, potentially, the whole. There is no such thing as a fraction; whatever might be considered a fraction has the totality potentially within it.

The physical world is the emergence within the framework of time and space of a reality that is originally what the ancients called "chaos" (although they used the term not to mean "disorderly," but quite the opposite). We might say that the physical world is simply the way that reality is focused. When reality comes into focus in the personal consciousness, we call it the physical universe, but most of the reality of the physical universe is unknown to us: it is implicit, not explicit. So although we often stress the importance of being in the here and now, the here and now is simply the framework through which the everywhere and always comes through in a transient way.

Human beings have the capability to defy time and space, and when we do so we are relieved of our fear of death and our fear of failure. At these moments, we discover our eternity—and we also discover that we ourselves are potentially the totality. For example, a common experience in meditation is the realization that the body is actually created from the fabric of the universe, out of which it arises just as a wave arises out of the sea. A further realization is that the wave does not arise out of the sea: it is the sea that emerges as a wave. With this realization, the meditator can see that the body is the fabric of the universe that emerges in a particular location. Our everyday sense of ourselves circumscribes us within a frontier or boundary that is purely in the mind. The very words "I" and "me" are a mystification—the great delusion. This is the real meaning of the Hindu concept of *maya,* the illusion with which we live all the time—and then we wonder why things happen the way they do.

This is why picking problems to bits under a microscope, which is called psychoanalysis, can never provide the total picture. The psychologist tends to fall into a subtle kind of dialectic, in which he tries to manipulate the patient to confirm his own preconceived ideas, and when he is engaged in this process, he is naturally not open to all the richness that is coming through the person.

Psychosynthesis, as opposed to psychoanalysis, would give a more holistic view of the problems of the patient. The word "holistic" is closely related to the word "whole" as well as to the word "holy"; the idea was first introduced by General Smuts when he said that the whole is greater than the sum of the parts. It is not enough to pick a problem to pieces; we must see all the dimensions behind the problem. Analysis may be valid for diagnosis, but therapy is much more important than diagnosis. Analysis is cause-oriented, whereas therapy is purpose-oriented. In analysis, the patient is considered as an "It," as in the "I-It" relationship described by Martin Buber. When the patient is considered as "Thou," true communication begins to take place.

The purpose of therapy is, of course, to help, and there can be no preconceived ideas about what is helpful. Not only psychotherapists but all people are called upon to be what might be called "backbench" therapists or counselors. People turn to other people in desperation, and we all seem to think we know better how to run others' lives than they themselves do: we are all ready to give advice. If we knew how much harm we can do by giving advice, particularly by telling other people what to do, we would realize that we have damaged the lives of many people. It is impossible to know all the aspects of other people's problems, even if they are not masquerading, mystifying themselves, or presenting a view of their problems that the listener might be impressed with, as is so often the case. In giving advice, there is a tendency to jump to conclusions; and a person in desperation is only too ready to take whatever advice is offered. On the other hand, a child about to endanger its own life must be stopped or warned, and, in a sense, there is no way not to influence another person, because we are all interacting with one another: one's very silence may constitute a message.

We would like, therefore, to consider what might be behind the problem that has been brought to us. It may be that a person has a problem because he finds himself placed in a situation in which he has to make an effort to overcome something in himself. By telling him what to do, we take away the possibility that the divine programming is offering him to perfect himself; and, of course, if things go wrong it is the adviser who will be blamed.

To help other people, what is really needed is intuition. A young man once came to me in desperation, saying he was being unjustly treated. He had been accused of setting fire to a hospital. When I looked at him, he seemed to be a perfectly nice young man, and he looked me straight in the eyes with an air of total innocence. For a moment, I really thought that he was being misjudged, although there was something behind his look of innocence that did not seem to be entirely clear. Instead of judging him by the evidence he gave me, I went into meditation in his presence, and in that state was able to experience my deepest reaction to the state of his spirit—to feel, as it happened, my own guilt in contact with him. I looked him in the eyes and said, "I know that you did it," and he broke down and confessed.

This kind of immediate evaluation cannot be made unless the practitioner can rely entirely on his or her intuition. The ordinary methods of psychoanalysis might be able to break down the masking of the soul, but it is a difficult and lengthy path; the use of intuition makes it possible to pinpoint a problem instantly, with great clarity. Trying to sort things out with the mind makes it difficult, if not impossible, to reach right into the soul of a person and to discern the motivations that are beyond the ordinary motivations of the mind.

As therapists, then, we would like to develop intuition, which is simply the word we use to describe an uncanny hunch we might have about things, which seems to be contradicted by our normal, rational thinking but is confirmed later on. There are, of course, various types of intuition. In the spiritual tradition of the East, there are many stories about intuition. For example, I was once the guest of the son of the president of Pakistan, and asked him if he could show me where I might find a dervish—a mystic of the Sufi tradition. He said, "Just follow this road, then turn right; there's a banana stand there, and in it is an old man wrapped in a blanket. He's a great king, but he's there among the banana peels." I asked why the young man could not take me there, and he replied, "Oh, no—the last time I went to see him he cursed me, and I was so distraught that I had an accident and broke my leg. But," he added, "if I hadn't broken my leg I would have gone on the first flight of Air Pakistan, of which I am president, and that flight crashed." I asked, "Well, if he saved your life by cursing you, why don't you let yourself be cursed a number of times?" He, however, declined.

In fact, it is not uncommon to find that people are afraid of dervishes. The methods of the dervishes are often very strange, and sometimes their power is so great that they say,

"Don't come anywhere near me, because I will burn you."
But there was a woman dervish, Hazrat Babajan, who said,
"You cannot reach your destination without passing by me,
and you cannot pass by me without looking into my eyes;
and you cannot look into my eyes unless you are totally
truthful, so you must choose." There is also a story of a
dervish who, while simply walking down the street, could
see into the hearts of all the people he encountered and tell
them everything about themselves in precise detail. He
could do this because he was totally unaware of time and
space. He didn't know who he was; he had lost his own
sense of identity, and therefore was able to reach into an
overall consciousness—the consciousness of the cosmos. We
all might very well like to be endowed with that kind of
intuition, and the truth is that we are; we are simply unaware of our intuition and how to bring it out.

To understand the consciousness of the cosmos, through
which we can bring out our intuition, we can make a comparison. If we imagine the consciousness of a bee, we might
find that the consciousness of the beehive is stronger in the
individual bee than its own personal consciousness. In the
same way, when our own sense of identity spills over the
border that we assign to our person, we have access to the
collective consciousness (which is not the same thing as the
collective unconscious). This phenomenon accounts for such
eerie occurrences as the awareness many women have of the
moment their husbands die on the battlefield during a war,
or the particularly uncanny link between a child and its
mother: if a child makes the slightest whimper, its mother
will awaken even if she is able to sleep on undisturbed
through much louder noises from other sources.

There have been numerous experiments investigating the
ability to transmit messages in an uncanny way, and generally in these experiments it turns out that the receiver of the
message is producing mostly alpha and theta brainwaves,

which are often associated with meditative states. It is most likely that if we could hook up the dervishes I have described here to an electroencephalogram machine, we would find that they were producing a great many theta and perhaps even delta brainwaves when they were in the state of cosmic consciousness.

Often when we sink into a state of reverie, we are less centered in our personal consciousness than we are in ordinary waking states. We then find ourselves unable to intervene in the course of our thoughts, because there is a very strong link between consciousness and volition or will. The images that form in the mind in some states of reverie seem rather random, which, in fact, poses the problem of randomness in the universe. Randomness seems to appear in entropy, in decay. In the realm of biology, life is built up: What biologists call "information" is built up in the genetic code of life, and information is negentropy. There is no randomness; there is only trial and error, because at times the programming of nature finds itself lost in a blind alley, retraces its steps, and finds a better way of doing things.

The same process occurs in the images experienced in reverie. There is a certain amount of waste in our thinking, just as there is waste from the food in the body, and this waste becomes apparent in the process of digestion that takes place in our thinking—a process that takes place all the time, but particularly during sleep. In a state of reverie, we experience something of what we experience when we are asleep, so we can watch the apparently random thoughts and wonder whether they make any sense; we try to project our sense of meaningfulness upon a process that can never be limited to our sense of meaningfulness. There is waste, or a dispersal, but there are also meaningful images that emerge from the meaningless ones. Picking out these creative images from the images that are just feedback from the environment is simply a matter of focusing the consciousness.

Our thinking is a mixture of many different elements, but we can outline two major factors in it: the feedback from the environment and creative thinking. The feedback from the environment constitutes the impressions we are exposed to —an accident we may have come across, a conversation, a book: thoughts are fed into our minds, and we then try to classify or pigeonhole them. When we have creative thoughts, we seem to be tapping a source that is unknown to us. The inspiration of a musician or artist seems to come from a super-mind, or the planning behind the universe. The phrase "the planning behind the universe" does not imply that everything has been predestined from the beginning of time; the planning behind the universe is always spontaneous, inventive, and exploratory. That is why there is trial and error. What is truly extraordinary is that we are part of that planning. In fact, because there are no boundaries to our being, we *are* that planning. This is what endows us with creativity.

In a state of reverie, we do not limit our thoughts to our preconceived ideas, and consequently creative thoughts can come through, but they do tend to get mixed up with all the other thoughts that emerge in that state, which are random. What the dervish does is to pick up the creative images and sort them out, bringing about order in reverie, following the principle of "order out of disorder." The dervish is able to do this because he has lost his sense of identity—his sense of time and space—so that he is functioning in a way that is not what might be called conducive to life in the world. This raises the question of whether it is possible to live very much in space and time and still develop intuition. In fact, I believe that we should have our feet on the earth, our heads in the heavens, and our hearts beating with an excess of ecstasy; so the example of the dervish is not perfect, but only an example that will help us understand how to develop intuition. To determine whether we can do so while dealing with everyday life, we have only to resolve the question of whether it is possible to function on several planes at the same time—to be in what I call "stereoscopic consciousness." My answer is a resounding "Yes."

There are times when we feel completely at one with the whole universe. This happens particularly when we are young and romantic and are lying in the grass looking into the sky and feeling a part of all things, as if the frontiers between ourselves and the totality had disappeared. This is the most elementary form of mystical experience. At other times, when we are crossing the road or answering telephones, we feel very conscious of time and space. I know from my own experience that we can indeed combine these two different settings of consciousness, because I once subjected myself to an experiment at the Himalayan Institute in which my brain was producing theta waves, which are normal in sleep, and yet I was able to hear a conversation and later recall it. It is a not-at-all-uncommon experience to be asleep and at the same time be conscious of the cars in the street and even of one's own judgment or overview of what is heard or experienced, while simultaneously there are random thoughts associated with reverie. In this state, the consciousness does not try to "zoom in" on the random thoughts, but is offset from them; nevertheless, there is still some kind of subliminal awareness of the random thoughts. This might be called a twilight state of consciousness. As the species *Homo sapiens* evolves, we will develop more and more the ability to combine many different types of settings of consciousness at the same time. This is the objective of the holistic age.

Chapter 2:

THE COSMIC DIMENSION OF CONSCIOUSNESS AND THE THINKING OF THE TOTALITY

In the "twilight area" of consciousness that William James described as the field of consciousness surrounding the highly illuminated spotlight of personal consciousness, we can distinguish two dimensions, similar to latitude and longitude: the cosmic dimension and the transcendent dimension.

The cosmic dimension is revealed in the ability to enter into the consciousness of others. We can actually enter into the experience of others; the growth of our being comes by learning, not from the behavior of others, but from our experience of them. There is much more osmosis between people than is generally realized. The person who could be described as "uptight" is actually closing himself in to his own ego center and is, therefore, not enriching his being. He becomes judgmental of other people, and he becomes judgmental because he sees the other person at an "It."

It is not possible to understand things from the vantage

point of the personal self, the lens-like aspect of our consciousness, because that image of the panorama is so terribly impoverished. When we are able to experience ourselves as other beings, our experience is much richer, and this is something we can develop in time. It is only because we do not realize that we have access to the consciousness of other beings that we try to reach them through their outer shell —to communicate with them through their bodies or minds. Most people walking in a forest would see only the bark and leaves of the trees—and yet Saint Francis experienced what it was like to be a tree.

In the realm of physics, one of the most baffling phenomena now being investigated—which was foreseen by Albert Einstein—is that when two paired electrons are separated and one spins to the right and the other to the left, if the spin of one is changed, the spin of the other changes simultaneously. The electrons communicate in some way that is beyond time and space, and physicists have been unable to determine how one electron "knows" that the spin of the other has been changed.

Human beings can also communicate from consciousness to consciousness directly, without passing through time and space. We can use an analogy here: there is a difference between the experience we can have of our toes by looking at them and the experience we have of our toes by feeling them. To look at our toes, we have to pass through time and space; to feel them, we experience them through the total consciousness of the body. In the same way, we can communicate directly with the consciousness of another person by entering into the total consciousness of the universe, which includes the consciousness of the other person. The electron does not communicate with its partner: the total consciousness of the universe is affected by the change of the spin of one electron. We err when we think in terms of expanding "our" consciousness into all beings; in fact, we can only let our consciousness be correlated with the total consciousness. This is a phenomenon often described by mystics, and is, in fact, at least one of the dimensions of what we understand by God.

The best credo of all times is that of modern physics—that everything is an unbroken, undivided wholeness. That is the meaning of "La illaha illa 'llah hu" ("Nothing exists save God"), of "Shema Israel, Adonoi elohenu, Adonoi Ech'od" ("Hear, O Israel, the Lord thy God, the Lord is One")—the affirmation of oneness. It is the meaning of the Buddhist principle of "anata"—that there is no such thing as multiplicity.

It is our assumption that we are a fragment of the totality that stands in the way of our experiencing the totality. From the moment we can overcome that way of thinking, we have access to the thinking of the totality. That is intuition: experiencing what is happening to another person. One of the ways we can do this is to overcome the idea that we are located in space. That idea is a very basic assumption; in fact, at one time people wondered where the soul was—whether it was in the heart, the brain, or elsewhere—as if the soul could be located anywhere. People may no longer think about the location of the soul, but there is still a tendency to think of ourselves in terms of occupying a location in space. We can best overcome our sense of being encapsulated in a location in space by realizing that the totality of the universe emerges in specific ways in specific locations— but it is still the totality that emerges. From the moment we realize this, it becomes much easier to enter into the consciousness of all people.

Nature does, of course, build in a limitation on our ability to "tune in" to the entire cosmos. We can imagine the confusion that would ensue if our radios could not be tuned to a single station at a time, but were always open to all the frequencies. If consciousness were not centered in the individual—in the notion of self—we would be exposed to too many impressions to be able to process them. This is why our consciousness tends to be focused in the vantage point of the person.

It takes a greater capacity of our being to be able to encompass the experience of all beings and process it into an overall picture. This is, perhaps, why we do not seem to be able regularly to practice this art. We seem to have to oscillate our consciousness between the very highly centered personal consciousness and the overall, mystical state, which is limited to the time we are sitting in our own caves, or rooms, to meditate. What we would like to do is find a way to meditate in everyday life, so that we do not have to open one door only to close another. The only way to do this is to increase our capacity, so that we can both maintain the focal center of the person and, at the same time, have an overall consciousness. This overall consciousness is something that is always present in our consciousness, but we can increase it to a very large extent. It is this overall consciousness that allows us to get into the consciousness of all beings. In the sequel to Raymond A. Moody, Jr.'s book *Life After Life, Reflections on Life After Life* there are accounts of people who have "died" clinically and then come back to life. One of the experiences they reported having had while "dead" was entering into the consciousness of the people they had victimized. We can imagine what it might be like for a Nazi *Gauleiter* to enter into the consciousness of the people he had tortured: from that moment, he could never be the same again.

This point is particularly relevant to something we must go into very deeply: guilt. There are no limits to guilt. As one grows older—assuming that we become more sensitive as we evolve—one's sense of guilt increases. As awareness grows, we become more aware of the harm we have done to people, and thus must reckon with guilt more rather than less. If we get into the consciousness of beings we have unwittingly wronged, we will be aware of things we were not aware of before. Cosmic consciousness makes this possible, so we might say that the cosmicizing of consciousness has as one of its effects an increased awareness of the harm one has done to people.

When we conduct retreats in the manner of the Sufis, we always begin with purification of the heart rather than with the traditional ablutions. By purification of the heart, we mean the examination of conscience. In the same way, in counseling it is often not good enough to deal with the consciousness of patients; it is particularly important to deal with the conscience. The reason why many people are not dancing with joy is that they are weighed down by their consciences. It is very difficult to abandon oneself to participation in the cosmic celebration in the heavens when one is weighed down by a sense of guilt. And no one can say that he has no guilt, because there is no end to it. If people are being tortured right now in concentration camps, we are responsible, because we can in fact do something about it. If we could not do anything about it, we would not be responsible, but from the moment we know about the work of, for instance, Amnesty International, we know that we can do something about it, however limited our contribution may be. It is inexcusable to sit down to a meal and enjoy our lives when we have not written a letter on behalf of a prisoner of conscience or done something to alleviate the plight of children dying of hunger in the impoverished countries of the world.

To return to the cosmic dimension of meditation, which, as we have said, is related to space and our sense of being located in space, we can examine some methods for overcoming this idea. One method is to imagine that we are traveling our consciousness around a tetrahedron or a crystal that is suspended from the ceiling. Once we realize that we can look at it from several angles, we realize that we are not limited in our consciousness by the location that we occupy in space. Or we might look at a flower and then imagine what it might be like to be that flower, or get into the consciousness of our own dog and imagine what we would look like to our dog.

The Sufis say, "I see him through his eyes." Normally, we see others through our own eyes, but this posits seeing them through their own eyes. The corollary is, "I see myself through his eyes." At this point, our way of looking at things is multiplied by getting into the consciousness of all beings: our *imago animae*—our image of ourselves—is totally modified, because it is being lighted up from all sides. We identify ourselves with an image that we make ourselves. At first, we create that image ourselves, and then we get other people to concur with the image; and to some extent, we are disappointed if people do not concur with the image we make of ourselves. We tend to be very upset when we feel that we have been unjustly assessed, even though any assessment is purely relative. But if we were able to see how people look upon us, we would not be caught up in a definite image of ourselves, because our image of ourselves would be much more fluid, much richer, and much more composite.

In counseling, we often find that the ability of people to deal with their problems is limited by their idea of the situation and their idea of themselves—the *image mundi* and the *imago animae.* Both, of course, are false: the map is not the territory. The image we have of the circumstances is not the way things are, it is just the idea we have of the circumstances. The patient is caught in this idea. He is not free because he is limited by his assessment of the situation and his false image of himself. Farid ad-din Attar says, "O man, if only you knew that you are free. It is your ignorance of your freedom that is your captivity." Being exposed to the assessment of other people may not necessarily give us a true image of ourselves, but it will certainly add to the image we make of ourselves. This is of utmost importance, because one of the ways in which we limit ourselves most is by creating a particular notion of ourselves. That is our prison.

COSMIC CONSCIOUSNESS MEDITATION

Imagine that you are a pilgrim, you have left the world behind and are loosening the invisible strings that are holding you back. You have reached a deep state in retreat, where you find you have become like a deer in the forest: you are so much a part of nature that your consciousness reaches into the consciousness of the trees and the flowers, the wind and the sun. This is cosmic consciousness: consciousness that is no longer centered in the person. Imagine walking in the forest and becoming totally immersed in the whole scene by losing your personal consciousness. You experience what it is like to be a tree, a bird, a butterfly, an insect, a snake, an animal, a rock. We know that consciousness does not have to operate from the vantage point of the body. You can experience yourself as a rock by getting into the consciousness of a rock, experience yourself as a dog by getting into the consciousness of the dog, experience yourself as a flower by getting into the consciousness of a flower, or experience yourself as a person you know by getting into the consciousness of that person.

You can begin by getting into the consciousness of a crystal. A crystal is a very special form of matter. In most matter, the molecules are rather randomly distributed, but where matter has become very purified, as in a mineral crystal like quartz, all of the molecules are disposed in absolutely geometrical constructs, some of them rather simple, others more complicated, but always strictly geometrical. This is because all the molecules pulsate at the same frequency, so that the optimal position in which they can be packed is orderly. If you could get into the consciousness of each molecule, you would fine that is has found a way of relating to the other molecules in a state of resonance—it is locked into a cosmic harmony. Inasmuch as there is any personal consciousness in the molecule, in the atom within the molecule, or in the electrons within the atoms, it is expressing a harmony far beyond its own volition, the cosmic harmony. It is simply fitting into the resonancy and continuing to pulse without any variation in time and space, as if time and space had been suspended. In this case, overall consciousness is more important than personal consciousness, there is very little personal consciousness, so the overall consciousness comes out more strongly in the form of what we might call the symphony of the spheres. You can experience what it would be like to be a crystal—that wonderful readiness to oscillate at the frequency it is supposed to oscillate at by the conjunction of forces.

Because of its oscillation, the crystal lends itself to the rays of the light of the sun passing through it; if you get into the consciousness of a crystal, you experience what it is like to be so much in sync with the cosmic harmony that you also become an instrument of the light of the universe. You feel yourself totally clear and luminescent, effervescent. It is really a sacrifice of freedom, initiative, complexity, variety, fluctuations from sclerosed order—except that if the crystal is exposed to the energy of light, then some of the electrons may tear themselves away from the sclerosed order and fluctuate, taking a certain amount of freedom by traveling away from their orbitals; when they run out of energy, they have to fall back again into their orbitals, and at that time they radiate light: they have been activated by light, and now they themselves radiate light. You can experience the moment of glory when an electron is able to free itself of that sclerosed order, and then the joy of itself giving off light as it falls back into place again. Our bodies are like that—are partly crystals—so getting into the consciousness of the crystal will enable us to get deeper into the mystery of the very fabric of the planet, of which we are part.

Now you can get into the consciousness of a flower. Here there is a much greater degree of consciousness because the very substance of the flower is organic: it does not have to subject itself to such rigid laws as the crystal. Each molecule has its own contribution to the cell; it is given much more free choice and responsibility in the whole, and is also able to understand something about the other molecules—how they all fit into a purpose. The consequence is that the consciousness of a flower as a whole is much more advanced. You can get into that consciousness, as a whole, while at the same time being conscious of all the cells and molecules, and then you will see how the flower is delighted by having an opportunity to manifest beauty, to display beauty; in fact, the beauty of the cosmos is coming through it. You can feel how this beauty manifests as form and as shades of color, and you may also experience how precarious the flower feels: it is short-lived, and it is delivered into the hands of the environment, so that it can suddenly become too cold and be frozen, or have too much heat from the sun, or suffer from a drought or be stepped on by animals or by people. It is very precarious, although it has so much to bring through, and the only way it can survive its precariousness is to produce perfume—to transmute its molecules into perfume, so they can continue to express its beauty when it can no longer survive in the form in which it was living before. Of course, the flower has divine consciousness. All the beauty, and also the power, that are coming through are beyond its own personal consciousness, and where the personal consciousness is not strong, then the divine consciousness comes through more strongly.

In the dog, personal consciousness is much stronger, so the divine consciousness gets a bit bogged down. It comes through as the dog's instinct—sometimes overwhelmingly. Here it is easier not only to experience him or her through his or her own eyes, but also to experience yourself through the eyes of the dog. What do you look like to a dog? He is so excited, so enthused by your intelligence, and he would so much like to understand why you do things the way you do. This is why he is capable of deferring to your judgement, which sometimes makes him look subservient. It is because he cannot quite grasp your intelligence, but knows, perhaps from experience, that your intelligence usually proves to be right, or to be operative. We must look very different in the eyes of a dog than the way we have become accustomed to picturing ourselves. If we can really see ourselves as we would look to a dog, or to a lion or some other animal, we would be adding a whole new dimension to our experience of ourselves and to our self-image.

Now you might try getting into the consciousness of a person—a friend, someone very close to you. Here, there are some reservations to make, and rightly so, because some people would not like other people to be able to know all they think or how they feel. This is because many of us were hurt when we were children: we've been laughed at. Perhaps we think that people might not value some of our thoughts or would even consider them objects of derision. We might feel that some of our feelings are so sacred that perhaps people would either not understand them or not value their sacred nature. It may have been the case that we have confided in another person and that person has betrayed our confidence, with disastrous consequences. In wartime, for example, keeping a secret can be a matter of life and death. If a person comes to us in confidence and reveals to us a secret of his soul, we have no right to shout it from the rooftops. This is why doctors are under the rule of professional secrecy. There are many reasons why some people would not like everyone else to be able to read right into their hearts and souls, or into their thoughts, and it would be an indiscretion to try to probe behind their curtains of privacy. This is a practice that you can carry out with human beings only if you choose a person who is so close to you that you feel that person would have no objection to your looking right into his soul. Of course, there are different levels of the beings that might be involved; there should be no objection to reaching into the higher consciousness of any person—to experience what that person is experiencing when he is in a very high state of meditation. Very often, the murshids, or Sufi teachers, call their pupils when they are in a very high state of meditation, because they want to share it. When one experiences something very beautiful, one wants to share it, particularly when it is an impersonal experience. So I suggest that you think about people who are very close to you—but try to get into their real being rather than their personalities. What would their sense of identity, their self-image, be if they really knew themselves as they truly are in their non-manifested being—that aspect of themselves that has not yet manifested in their personality? This is a most important practice for counselors, gurus, and lovers, because anyone who loves another person can make that love creative by helping the person to be what he is. The only way to do that is to discover the real person. Then that person will discover himself through your eyes, and you will help him to become what he is.

You can think about one person after another, and imagine them in a very high state of consciousness. Then try to get into their consciousness. That high state of consciousness is actually the real foundation or ground out of which the personality of the person has grown, just as a crystal grows out of its foundation; and that foundation is really impersonal. So when you get into the consciousness of a person in his highest state of consciousness, you cannot say that you are getting into his personal consciousness. What you are getting into is a cosmic or transcendent state that is coming through that person, right down into his personality. At the time when you are reaching him, you are really reaching into the cosmic dimensions behind the personality. That is why many Hindus and Sufis say, "I see God in him. All that I see is God." At that level, what you see is divine attributes coming through the person.

This is a practice that I recommend doing every day—getting into the higher consciousness of all the beings around one. The next half of it is to see how you appear to each person. If that person is in his or her higher consciousness, then he or she is able to assess the non-manifest in you, which is those qualities that are on their way into manifestation in your personality but that have not yet come through fully. You realize right away that the very perception that person has of your higher being hoists your consciousness into its higher regions and makes you aware of those qualities that are the essence of your being and are trying to come through your personality.

We now come to the more general attunement of the contemplative who is on retreat, walking through the forest, or even walking through the city. His consciousness is distributed throughout and around him, instead of being centered in his person. Instead of judging people or animals or trees from the vantage point of his person, his consciousness is everywhere in all beings. This attunement brings about ecstasy. You can sit with your back against a tree and experience how the tree feels with your back against it. This consciousness may reach beyond the planet into the sun; it is consciousness of the sun that makes the rishis and dervishes so powerful. They experience what it is like to be the sun. According to the Sufis, the sun is a being—Prince Hurakhsh, the archangel of the sun—who is burning himself in sheer bursts of energy and, because of that, giving life to the entire planetary system. The sun embodies a life-giving, energy-giving disposition. So if you get into the consciousness of the sun, you yourself become life-giving. Having experienced the condition of the sun, you become like the sun.

You can even go beyond the sun to the consciousness of the distant stars. Then you can begin to see yourself from the point of view of the cosmos. Einstein, for example, when he was pushing a stroller in New York, could see himself pushing that stroller. In the middle of the enormous, overwhelming motions of the stars, and seeing the planet Earth as being just a little grain of sand in the whole vast mechanism of the universe, he could see himself pushing a stroller in New York with reference to the whole majestic motion of the stars. This is how you can see yourself: instead of being the center of the universe yourself, or thinking, "My body has emerged from the universe," you can think, "It is the universe that emerges as my body." That is a different attitude altogether.

The Sufis say that you get into the consciousness that links all things together. What does a leaf know of another leaf of a tree, except through the fact that both of them are part of the consciousness of the total tree? A leaf cannot reach another leaf through space; it reaches the other leaf because it has access to the consciousness of the whole tree, which includes the consciousness of all the leaves. In the same way, you can reach all beings by getting into the consciousness of all the collective beings together, instead of trying to reach each being through your eyes, through space and time, from outside. You see the bark of the tree if you reach a tree through space and time, but you can reach into the consciousness of the tree from inside.

The practices we are doing lead to becoming immersed in the total consciousness of God in the universe—not the consciousness of God beyond existence, but right in existence. That is what the contemplative does when he turns his attention inside instead of outside. It is more difficult to experience the consciousness of the tree if at the same time you are aware of how it looks in time and space. If you close your eyes, and therefore discard your picture of the tree from the outside, it is easier to get into the consciousness of the tree from inside and to experience what the tree experiences. That is why it is easier to experience what a person is like when you are not sitting in the presence of that person talking, although you can sometimes experience what a person is like by sitting in his presence without talking and with closed eyes.

This is why, as Buddha says, the contemplative places a sentinel at the doors of perception and turns within. Of course, you must be very careful that you do not encapsulate yourself in your own person. What is aimed at is to discover the whole universe from inside. To begin with, you close your eyes, so that you are not picking up information through the senses any longer. If you do this, you will generally find yourself caught in your thoughts, so the next stage is to do with your thoughts exactly what you did with the perception of the objects around you. You consider the thoughts as being external to yourself. Generally, we adjust ourselves to the thought process, but here you have to offset consciousness from the thought process. The thoughts will continue to function, just as the objects around you keep on moving, but you don't pay attention to them. It is just as if you were able to find a space within that is quite different from the space without. Hazrat Inayat Khan, the founder of the Sufi Order, says that the perceptions of the physical world tend to pull one's consciousness to the surface; when one resists that, then one finds oneself immersed in the depth. In this inner space, you are in the collective consciousness of all beings. We are all communicating from inside.

All the radio waves in the universe interpenetrate one another at every point in space, whereas the electrons occupy separate spaces. The waves are all co-present at one point of space, which means that all reality that appears in different locations in space is co-present in the inner space, irrespective of location. You can find everything everywhere —or, perhaps more accurately, nowhere, since this reality is not found in the space that is outside. There is no being, no thought, no happening in the universe that you cannot tune into, because it is all co-present in the inner space. You cannot reach it by going anywhere or by turning outside through your senses; you can reach it only by turning inside and getting into the divine consciousness.

Chapter 3:

THE TRANSCENDENT DIMENSION: AWAKENING FROM PERSONAL CONSCIOUSNESS

The cosmic dimension is one dimension of spirituality; the other is the transcendent dimension. We can compare the transcendent dimension to the view we would have if we were flying over the streets of a city in a helicopter: from a great height, we can see the interrelationship between the streets, which we could not see while walking in them. The transcendent viewpoint is a way of looking upon problems without being involved in them, so as to be able to have a certain amount of perspective and see the interrelationships, which means seeing the meaningfulness behind situations. The word "meaningfulness" is of utmost importance, because our greatest problem is to discover meaningfulness in our lives.

The quest for meaningfulness breaks down into three categories. The first is that our actions are fulfilling—they are meaningful to us in the sense that we feel we are accomplishing something that is meaningful. The second is unfolding the potentialities in our being that are latent. Perhaps the greatest despair is caused by what people feel is the failure to become what they had hoped to become. This sense of failure is felt not so much in the area of accomplishing things as in what one has become oneself, which is much more important. The third category is the desire to understand why things happen the way they do; it is a thirst for understanding, because it is a cause of enormous grief in the soul to be subjected to situations that one does not understand, or to be unable to see the meaning of the whole life. The physical conditions in the German concentration camps of World War II were abominable, but what the people in them suffered from most was a sense of the loss of meaningfulness; they wondered how it could be possible that they should be living in a world where such things could happen. There was a fear of being abandoned in the hands of a universe that makes no sense. What we mean by "looking for God" is, in fact, looking for sense. Today, the question is not whether God exists or not, but whether everything ultimately makes sense, because God is the ultimate sense. Our minds are continually destroying our intuition of meaningfulness, so we are constantly fighting against our reason. The greatness of a human being manifests when he stands by what he knows in his higher realization even when he is faced with proof of the opposite from the point of view of his mind. This is the strength of faith.

Attaining the transcendent point of view is crucial to awakening, because awakening is realizing that one is caught in a perspective. If most of us were to think back to ten years ago, we would realize how lucky it is that what we wished for never happened—or what a pity it is that it did. Our realization means that at that time we were caught in a perspective, and it has taken us all this time to see it. If we could now gain a new vantage point upon our present lives, we could see the perspective in which we are caught now; so we might say that awakening is the ability to get out of our present perspective now, without waiting ten years.

The Buddha was particularly able to show exactly how people become desperate when they are caught in the perspective of their personal sense of themselves. For example, a person who says, "I can't live without that person, whom I love and who left me," is caught in a perspective. He refuses to live because he can only live in his little perspective, and declines to participate in the great festivities in the heavens and in the joy of life because he is caught in that perspective. So we can see the necessity for the freedom described by Buddha, which is the freedom from perspective.

There is, of course, fulfillment in involvement, so that human beings remain suspended on the horns of a dilemma —between involvement and freedom. When one is aware of one's eternity, one sees the importance of what is transient in relative terms. This gives some immunity against being caught in a perspective. The method used in the East for effecting this is to disidentify oneself with all the transient aspects of one's being—the body, the mind, the personality, and so forth. Our awareness of our eternity is already present in our intuition, so it is not terribly difficult to offset our consciousness from its identity with those aspects of ourselves that are transient and discover our eternal identity.

There are moments when we are aware of having always existed and aware that we will always exist. This awareness is also part of the awareness that we have always been and will always be as a continuity within change. It is not as if a part of our being were eternal and another part subject to change; our eternity is like an Ariadnean thread that runs through beyond the episode that is this life on earth. The experience of this eternity is one without which our whole sense of meaningfulness would collapse, because if it is true that what we experience in the episode we call our life is perishable, life would not make sense; and everything in life makes sense.

Whatever has been gained—what is called negentropy in physics—is transmitted further. What is meant by negentropy is the building up of information. Memory is the passage of the transient into the eternal: memory eternalizes an episode that was transient. This does not mean that one is the same person, but simply that there is continuity in change. The only way to experience our identity is to accept that we can be different from what we think we are now—to give up our sense of identity, suspending time and yet still hanging on to our present identity. This can be done in the practice of regression, in which we can look back into the episodes of life through childhood and even into the time when we were in the womb and beyond, experiencing the continuity of our being and therefore overcoming the sclerosis of the identity when we think we are the person we think we are. This is a practice that is very useful in therapy.

The cosmic dimension is linked with space; the transcendent dimension is linked with time. Physics has gone only so far in its examination of time. In relativity, there is only one dimension of time: time is accounted for in only one direction. But we can recognize two dimensions, one of which is becoming and the other of which is passage from transience to eternity.

The word "eternity," like the word "infinity," is very misleading. Instead of thinking of infinity as a thing we can grasp, we should perhaps consider it an infinite regress—something that is never reached. The idea of divine perfection poses the same problem: we tend to think in terms of the *eidos* of Plato, the perfect archetypes from which everything derives. If there is any meaningfulness in evolution, it is just because there is a continual perfecting going on. We mustn't imagine God as being perfect at the beginning of time, and that everything here is imperfect and striving to-wards perfection. Instead, we must realize that we are the being of God who is continually perfecting Himself: poten-tially perfect, in actuality not perfect. The preconceived ideas we have of eternity, infinity, and perfection (among other preconceived ideas) are straitjackets in which the souls of human beings become imprisoned and suffer alienation, suffocation, despair, and agony; and much of our agony is in the soul—what Heidegger called metaphysical anxiety.

We have to deal with these big issues because they are implicated in personal issues. People come to us with their problems; they want to know whether they should marry this person or that person, or whether they should get a divorce, or a new job, or move to another city. Perhaps they have trouble controlling their anger or an anxiety complex. There are innumerable practical and personal problems. But behind them all are the greater issues. Most often, a patient will try to draw the therapist into his problem, and then the therapist loses his ability to help him. This is where the transcendent dimension is invaluable, because it makes it possible for us not to judge situations according to face value or the bare facts. It makes it possible for us to see into the programming of the universe—to see what Hazrat Inayat Khan calls "the cause behind the cause and the purpose beyond the purpose."

These are two factors behind the facts: the cause and the purpose. Cause manifests in a chain of events, which in Buddhism is called *pratityasamutpada.* The causal chain could account for quite a number of things, such as how a person develops ulcers or cancer or schizophrenia: he may have been jammed in a situation in which he could not turn right or left, so something had to give—either the mind, so that schizophrenia developed, or, if the mind was fairly strong, the body, so that he developed cancer, which is an illness of the DNA—the programming of the body—or, less severely, ulcers. Or the experience of being jammed may have caused him suddenly to become aggressive or violent. It may be that one of the explanations for the terrible violence of our time is despair—doubt as to the meaningfulness of the programming behind life, which is a way of saying a lack of a belief in God.

The most wonderful thing that can happen is seeing into the meaningfulness of life. And the extraordinary thing is that we not only participate in our bodiness in the fabric of the universe, but we also have access into the thinking behind the universe. Indeed, we *are* that thinking: there is no frontier. This is the redeeming grace.

What I advocate here is not what I usually recommend—retiring into a room and practicing samadhi, which is an experience of raising one's consciousness beyond one's personal vantage point; what I am advocating is the development of the ability to look upon oneself objectively in the middle of action. Instead of entering into the consciousness of other beings and seeing how we look to them, we can practice disassociation of personality so that one dimension of our being is able to look upon another dimension of being. We might call this a second degree of awareness; as Teilhard de Chardin said, "The animal knows, but man knows that he knows." We can watch ourselves watching.

An example of an extreme case of disassociation of a personality is that of a woman who was practicing biofeedback and trying to produce theta waves. She reported that she was able to look upon her being "down there" in time and space, while she herself was "up there." She had disassociated herself with her spatial, temporal being and become the being who was "up there." When she decided she was able to get down into the being that was "down there" in time and space, the being that was higher seemed like a super-being with whom she could not totally identify. Her sense of identity changed when she slipped into the being who was in the spatial and temporal dimensions.

Stereoscopic consciousness is the ability to be in both of

34

these consciousnesses at the same time. It is easy to oscillate between the two, but to be in both at the same time is a great thing. We can even reach beyond the being "up there" to higher heights; we can not just know that we know, but know that we know that we know, into infinite regress. This is the real meaning of transcendence. It is what Hazrat Inayat Khan called divine consciousness. He said that when one is in divine consciousness, then one does not see facts except at the edge of one's reality; what is more important, one sees what is behind the facts. That is much more important than the facts, because facts are just the projection of reality that is temporal and spatial but not the essence of reality. In divine consciousness, one gets into the programming behind the universe.

This is why the psychotherapist must be an enlightened being. Otherwise, the "therapy" is like the blind leading the blind. This is why we are living in a time when so many psychotherapists feel they must take initiation into the state of awakening.

BUDDHIST SATTIPATANA AND JHANAS

Sattipatana is a Buddhist practice. In it, one does not cut out the consciousness of the physical world or the mind world—the world of thoughts—but one does not allow oneself to be caught in the perspective whereby one looks at the physical world through one's personal consciousness.

There are a few basic ways of looking at things that are the underlying core of Buddhism. The first is that suffering is due to ignorance: we are caught in a perspective, so what Buddha is doing is unmasking our ignorance. Freedom is not freedom from the physical world, but from being trapped in it. Sattipatana is not just blanking out the consciousness of the physical world, it is looking at everything without being fooled or trapped in it. The trap is desire—wishing for things —so the path of Buddhism is desirelessness. It is the path of the monk and the ascetic. Buddhism creates a totally impersonal, objective way of looking at things and unmasking the hoax that we are all caught up in.

Begin the practice of sattipatana by considering your body very objectively, without identifying with it, as though it were something you were observing. It is not the subject, but the object. You realize that it is made of the same substance as the trees, the grass, the clouds, the earth; in fact, it is a formation made out of the substance of the earth. It may have been elaborated in the course of evolution into something wonderful, but it is not you. How can you say it is you? You could not make it, and, anyway, what are "you"? What you mean by "me" could not be this extraordinary piece of machinery that has been worked out in so much detail. "Yes," you may say, "but I feel differently about this body than I do about the body of another person. At least, I may not be this body, but I entertain a very special connection with this lump of flesh." But by the very fact that you say, "I can see that I entertain a very special connection with this lump of flesh," you reveal the fact that you are able to disidentify with the body. And although you may not know what you mean by "I," at least you realize that you do not mean that you are your body. You have attained a degree of disinterestedness.

You can imagine walking in the forest and suddenly realizing that your body is made of the same substance as the woods, and you can make it walk! At that moment you are caught in the magic of life—of what life means. You realize that there had been confusion because you had thought that the body was you. When you have reached this degree of clarity, you can look upon the death of the body without fear, because it is not you anyway. It is a temporary forma-

36

tion that has a certain purpose. In fact, there is nothing more liberating than what the monks used to call *contemplatio mortis*—contemplating death—thinking of the body rotting under the earth and letting go of it, because if it was formed, then it must also be disintegrated.

"If I am not this body, what am I? Who am I?" What is a river? You imagine that it is the water, yet it is never the same water. You are like a river: a continuity of transient things. It is a very perplexing thought. Whatever you are is certainly not material, because the material aspect of the river is totally transient.

In the next stage, you look upon your mind and see that thoughts arise and thoughts call for other thoughts by a process of association; thoughts vanish and new thoughts arise. So thoughts are formations. You realize that these thoughts have been conditioned, just as your body has been programmed by the impersonal forces of evolution and is, in fact, part of the whole flow of bodiness of the universe. In the same way, your thinking has been programmed: it is the thinking of the universe. "Yes," you will say, "but I can decide to concentrate on one thought rather than another, just as I can decide to move my arm." So you do have some action upon the mind, and once more this confirms that you are not the mind. You have some influence on it, but you are not it. You can catch yourself believing that these are my thoughts when in fact you could not think differently, because it is the way your thinking has been programmed, and as long as you think it is your thinking you will be fooling yourself.

In the third stage, you contemplate your personality. You think you are made in a certain way—you have a lot of joy in you, or you have a bad temper, or a lot of beauty—whatever it is you think is your personality. "That's me, and you can see that I am different from that person, because that person has a totally different personality. I am my personality." But that personality you say you are has been inherited. In fact, it is a continuation of the personalities of your parents and grandparents, right back to the dawn of creation, so how can you say it is you? It is a product of the impersonal forces of nature, and it is continually growing and changing. You have some action upon your personality, just as you have on your body and your mind: you can encourage certain features in your character. When this becomes clear, you are robbed of your sense of identity with the personality, and you watch yourself reacting. You are built up in such a way; you have been programmed. Now you can look upon your personality as a vehicle that you are using, but that is not you. This gives you a tremendous freedom.

We now come to the most difficult stage. "I am not my body, I am not my mind, I am not my personality, so what am I? I must be my consciousness, because I perceive this, I realize this, I remember that. I am that which is aware; I am the subject." Yet this, too, must be negated as the most basic of all illusions. Buddha explains it this way: he says consciousness is like a flame, and the flame depends upon the combustible. As long as there is a log, there is a flame. Is that what you are? And is it the same flame that burns one log and then another? How can you say, "I am this consciousness or that consciousness"? You begin to realize that there is just consciousness, and that consciousness emerges when a formation has been built up. There is consciousness flowing through a crystal, but you cannot say that it is the consciousness of the crystal. Then you become aware of the total consciousness of the universe. You have been systematically robbed of your sense of identity: you realize that your body is embedded in the total universe, your mind is embedded in the thinking of the total universe, your personality, which you thought was a clear hallmark of yourself, is part of the bounty of qualities manifested everywhere,

and your consciousness, which you thought was the very
epitome of yourself, is totally implicated in the whole consciousness of the universe. Your sense of identity has kept
on moving backward, and now you identify with the universal consciousness, totally impersonally.

These are the four stages of sattipatana leading toward
freedom and awakening. Once you have gone through the
four stages of sattipatana and consciousness is not limited
within the vantage point of the person, the whole physical
world looks totally different. For example, from the point of
view of the consciousness threaded through the lens of the
person, the stars look like points in the sky and the sun
seems to turn around the earth. That is the way the universe
appears to us, but that is not the way the universe is. We are
caught in a very narrow view of the universe. The picture
we have of the universe is a very far cry from the reality of
the physical universe: it is just a picture. We are caught in
an illusion, and we are so convinced of it that we argue about
it and act on the strength of this image that we make of the
universe.

If you refer everything to your sense of yourself as a
person, that is the reason why you do not see things as they
are. The reason is that the eyes are programmed in such a
way as to refer everything to the eyes. But if instead of
contacting the physical universe through your senses you
got into the consciousness of the trees and the rocks and the
animals and the people, then imagine how different the
universe would look. If you were able to reach out with your
consciousness into outer space, you would realize that the
stars are enormous and that the planets that you cannot even
see from the planet Earth are enormous. That is the kind of
state you are in when you are high. Suddenly, space relationships are altered, and you discover a totally different
way of experiencing the universe. You get into direct contact
with the universe by eliminating your image of it.

We do communicate with the universe through our senses limited through the personal vantage point, but we can communicate with the universe without being limited by the senses. We can do both: we can walk in the forest, and our eyes may be aware of how the trees look, but we can also experience a transfigured universe—experience what it feels like to be those trees at the same time that we are seeing them. We are communicating with them through our senses, and simultaneously we are communicating with them in a deeper way. Consciousness is partly functioning without being limited by its focalized center. For example, the ant may be partly operating from its personal vantage point and partly from the consciousness of the total ant nest. This is what Buddha calls the first jhana: a totally different relationship with matter. From the moment one unmasks the hoax and sees clearly that one's idea of the universe is not the universe, one begins to communicate with the universe directly. It is a stupendous experience: suddenly you realize that you have let yourself be fooled.

In the second jhana, you begin to enter into the thinking behind the physical universe instead of just assuming that the physical universe is reality. You realize that what appears as physical is just a crystallization of thoughts. Even the subatomic particles are the thinking of the universe that is manifested in a tangible way. It affects our retina, for example, but it could not exist without the thought that it incorporates. It is thought, materialized thought. A cell of the body is a thought that is proliferating, pulsing, and moving.

You discover the thinking of the universe, and you realize that you yourself are part of the thinking of the universe, so your connection with the physical universe is very different. When you see a tree, you don't think, "Well, this is a tree, a physical tree"; and when you enter into the consciousness of the tree, you enter into the consciousness of the thought that manifests in its physicalness the thinking behind the physical universe. Then you can see very well that if you are only conscious of your thinking, you cannot be conscious of the thinking of the universe, and you can see that it is the notion of yourself as an individual that stands in the way of the vastness of your experience. You are being caught in a limitation, and the way of Buddhism is freedom from all limitations. It is the notion of the self that is a limitation: the more you are able to let go of your assumption of being a person, the more you are able to be aware of the thinking of the universe. When you become conscious of yourself, you get enclosed in your personal thinking—or the part of the thinking of the universe that is enclosed in that section of the totality.

In the third jhana, Buddha goes one stage further into the emotions behind the universe. He sees people everywhere being caught in personal emotions, thinking that situations are the way they are, and being happy if they think the situation is good and sad if they think the situation is bad. Yet, as Hazrat Inayat Khan says, a defeat might prove to be a victory, and what seems to be a victory might prove to be a defeat. Our emotions are part of the way we see things. For instance, if your lover has left you, you feel terrible. It might be the best thing that could have happened, but if you are caught in your personal point of view, it seems like a terrible tragedy. You are caught in an appearance, and your emotions are all caught up in the appearance, because you are caught in a very limited perspective. If you could see from a vaster perspective, your emotions would be totally different.

Once you get into the consciousness of the emotions of the universe, your own emotions do not seem important anymore. For example, how can you be jubilant about being elected president of your club when you know that people are being beaten to death in concentration camps? And how can you be depressed because you have lost five thousand dollars when you are aware of the jubilation in the heavens? When consciousness reaches into the vastness and you see that everywhere there is emotion—vulgar, sadistic, selfish, self-sacrificing, jubilant, serene—you can even see that, in a way, a person is his emotions.

From the time you overcome the notion of self, you overcome personal emotions like hatred or selfishness or self-satisfaction, and you see that many emotions, which might be called lower emotions, are related to the fulfillment of desire. These emotions attune you to a certain pitch, and keep you at that pitch. When you are desireless, emotions become very sublime, and your love for all people becomes very beautiful. There is a chemistry of emotions: you are passing from the more lush emotions to the frigid emotions, like the emotions of a nun or the Virgin Mary—very pure, impersonal, and serene. If you want to get into the consciousness that is the emotion of the Buddha, the emotion that manifests as his being, you cannot see him giggling, or even laughing; he smiles, but he does not laugh. And you cannot see him breaking into tears of personal suffering: he has no personal emotions. He is experiencing the emotion of the cosmos, which he calls "the healing of the wounds." We suffer because we desire, and this is the way to overcome suffering and to be free, free from the self. If you get into the consciousness of Buddha, you cannot be stirred by personal emotions. You see them, and you can help another person overcome them by the fact that you have overcome them yourself. Your peace becomes contagious and helps people overcome their personal sorrow. We can well understand that Buddha said, "I have found the way to overcome personal suffering."

In the fourth jhana, consciousness is carried beyond the

notion of self. So long as we think, "What am I conscious of? I am conscious of this physical world. Actually, now I realize that it is just my image of the physical world, and now I can also be conscious of remembering something that happened when I was two years old, but consciousness has been interrupted at my birth," we are at the edges of consciousness. If consciousness spills over the edges of the person, you will remember right back to the life of your ancestors; you will remember previous incarnations; you will remember the planes through which you passed on the descent to the plane of incarnation. In fact, not only will you get back the memory of all those things that might have been communicated physically by our parents and ancestors, or nonphysically at the level of reincarnation, but you will also remember the whole past of the universe. What is more, you will be aware of all the planes and all the beings of all the planes.

If your consciousness is not limited to your sense of yourself, your vantage point will extend and encompass the whole universe. That is the great victory, the moment of illumination, that Buddha experienced at the end of the forty-nine days he spent under the bodhi tree: consciousness spills over the frontiers of the man sitting under the tree and reaches right out into the whole past, into a panoramic view of the whole past, all levels of angelic beings, universes beyond universes—the whole breathtaking vision beyond the physical universe. This is the way out of the prison of the little environment and the little personal emotions. What Buddha sees is universes being formed, growing, proliferating, and exploding; and then other universes replacing them. (This tallies with what we learn in science about the universe expanding and contracting, about other universes beyond the one we are aware of, and about black holes, white holes, and so forth.) When we start reaching beyond what we generally experience, we realize that there is no end. That is what happened to the consciousness of Buddha: it reaches into realms a person caught in his personal consciousness could never dream of.

Buddha even gives us a clue: he says that all we have to do is to identify with the mode of reality corresponding to the level that we want to reach, and then we will experience that level. If you identify with the body, wherever you go you see bodies; people are bodies for you. If you identify with the personality, wherever you go you will be communicating with personalities. If you identify yourself with your thinking, you will be communicating with the thoughts of people. But if you identify yourself with a being of light, everywhere you go you will be seeing the light— the reality of light behind the physical aspect of things. You will discover the world of light.

Buddha speaks about realms that are beyond existence, and then he goes beyond consciousness. When we are conscious of a physical object, or of a thought, or of a cause, there is duality between consciousness and the object. In samadhi, there is no dichotomy between subject and object; there is only awareness without an object. Those are the realms beyond existence. Buddha includes the state of samadhi in his experience, but he does not exclude the physical universe in this vast panoramic experience. His final words before he died were, "That which had to be done has been done"; and then he said, "This is the cessation of the determined." Your body and mind are determined by the environment, but when you reach the state of awakening, you have overcome causality, and that means that you are totally free.

Chapter 4:

SPIRITUAL DIMENSIONS OF EMOTION

On retreat, people go through different stages or states, and the same thing is true in life. It would be helpful in dealing with people who come to us for counseling to be able to outline what state they are in.

In a retreat, which may last from three to forty days, we follow a schedule that is based upon the alchemical stages in the *ars regia*—the royal art—described by Jung in his book *Psychology and Alchemy.* Jung describes the states of the alchemical process, which the Sufis call *maqamat* and which promote transformation. Our objective is transformation. We cannot solve another's problem for him, but we can promote forward movement in that person; the problem is like a handicap—a pothole or a snare—on the way toward progress.

The first stage is total dislocation of one's notions. One's notions of the environment, of the situation, and of oneself disintegrate as a result of going through what Saint John of the Cross called the dark night of the soul. This is a state that could lead to schizophrenia, so it is important for anyone facing the disruptive forces of nature, which always tend to destroy things before recreating them, to have something to hang on to. The assumptions, emotions, and thoughts generally gravitate around the notion of the personal self, so when a person is going through a "dark night," the ultimate disassociation or dislocation is of the sense of the ego—not necessarily the qualities of the personality, but the sense of being a person, an individual.

At this point, it is important to be able to carry oneself into the second stage, where one begins to identify oneself with a higher level of one's being than one has so far done. This is the transcendent level: one may experience oneself as being a continuity in change while overcoming the limited sense of being a person. One experiences oneself as being nameless and formless and spaceless and timeless. It is the discovery of one's eternity.

In third stage, which is the ultimate stage in the ascent, one discovers oneself as being pure spirit and pure intelligence. One is not aware of the physical plane or the images of the mind, so it is a stage that is very similar to deep sleep without dreams; consciousness has been resolved in its root, which is intelligence. What is more, in this stage one touches upon the fountainhead of energy, the catalyst of all energy, which is spirit. The third factor one experiences is ecstasy, which is neither joy nor pain, but something beyond them both—and, of course, beyond description. The ascent has gone beyond the actual world into the world of reality at the same time that it has become formless, timeless, spaceless, ethereal, and impersonal; at the very top, there is only the awareness of being not *an* intelligence, but intelligence; not *a* spirit, but spirit, experiencing not personal joy but cosmic ecstasy—the celebration in the heavens.

After having gone through the stages of the ascent, one goes through the stages of the descent, in which one intervenes, or participates, in one's own rebirth—the building up out of that which was scattered. This culminates in the alchemical betrothal or wedding, which is a coalescence of all the elements that one has accrued into a much greater, new sense of being a person. This is very important, because we do not wish to become impersonal, like the dervish, but rather to be able to bring impersonal dimensions into the person.

The ultimate state, which is the consummation of the whole process, is what the alchemists call the spiritualization of matter and the materialization of spirit. One is able to coordinate all the different factors experienced, so that one can, for instance, experience oneself as the divine perfection functioning in limitation; as Hazrat Inayat Khan said, "Man is divine limitation, and God is human perfection."

Before anyone can even enter the first stages, however, it is necessary to face two things: guilt and despondency. If we go on retreat, we have to leave the world behind, like pilgrims. That means we must learn a certain amount of detachment from the invisible strings that hold us back, and know how to give expression to that aspect of our being that is the hermit. In all of us, there is a compromise, or dichotomy, between the hermit and the knight.

The most insidious of the invisible threads linking us with the so-called outer world is the feeling of having a bad conscience about something one has done to somebody. One may even have been responsible for a real disaster, or done something willfully and intentionally that has caused unnecessary pain. One may even have a bad conscience about a situation in which which one had no alternative but to cause another person pain. Whatever the reason, there may still be a feeling of guilt, even if the action can be justified in the mind. There is also the guilt of not having acted in a situation to save others from loss or pain. If a house is burning and no one is home, and we do not take the responsibility for calling the fire department, we are responsible for further damage to the house; if a child is about to do something dangerous, it is our responsibility to protect him or her. Everyone is under our care. We may even feel guilt for turning away the beggar at the door.

Our objective is to be free, but in order to be free we must go deeply into the opposite of freedom: despair, suffering, and grief. Detachment can be simply failing to face responsibility, and we can never attain real freedom unless we face responsibility. The problem is how to transmute personal suffering into joy. Many people would prefer simply to turn away from suffering; they go to parties, turn on the television, or dance to rock'n'roll—anything not to be aware of the suffering in the world. There is enough suffering as it is, and people do not want to get too involved in it. That is not facing it; and even the sannyasin who puts on a yellow robe and leaves the world cannot be totally free, because he is not facing the problems of people.

This is a problem that is frequently encountered: the need to be free, and, with it, the terrible fear that we have curtailed our freedom by involving ourselves with people and situations. There is no way we can ever be free without being cruel, and since we do not feel like being cruel, we just accept our prison. But sometimes we can be more free when we are bound than when we are free externally and bound internally. At least, we cannot attain freedom by turning away from the world or from responsibility or from our own guilt.

How can we attain freedom when we are weighed down by guilt? There are some cases in which we can do something about it; for example, we can write a letter to the person we have wronged. It can be an extraordinary experience for a person after twenty years to receive a letter saying, "I apologize—I feel that I have done you wrong." In that case, we have outweighed suffering by trying to mitigate it, and we have helped the person to believe in the meaningfulness of life and the goodness of the human species. We may even have redeemed him from the hell of recrimination that he may have been carrying all that time in his heart.

If the person we have wronged has died or cannot be located, we mustn't think that there is nothing we can do to repay the harm we have done. It is not like a bargain: there is no way to measure it. But we can still do something, without ever assuming that we are able to pay back what was done; what we have done is irrevocable, and, indeed, it is the irrevocable nature of our actions that makes them so traumatic in our unconscious minds.

One way we can overcome the despair of guilt is to see the cause behind it. Perhaps we were part of a whole network of situations, and perhaps we were the stick with which God had to hit that person, or nudge that person in the direction in which he was supposed to be going. It is very unfortunate that one was chosen to be that, but perhaps karma, which is personal responsibility, is much more scattered, or collective, than we might think. If we could see behind the whole programming of the universe, we would know that it had to be the way it was. This is a very difficult proposition to make, because if things are the way they are supposed to be, then there would be no point in trying to change anything; only a fatalistic attitude would be appropriate. What we want is not a fatalistic attitude, but the point of view of the person who has resurrected and who looks back upon the past and sees how everything came into place—not following a preconceived plan, but all working into place. It is a retrospective view.

In other words, there are different frameworks; one can look at the same situation through different frames of reference. From the personal point of view, one does have a responsibility. But, the situation being irretrievable, there is still something to do, which is to transform suffering into joy. In fact, we cause suffering to other people by our suffering; there is a snowballing effect. One's act has created anguish and remorse in oneself, and now it is spilling over onto other people, so the harm spreads. And, what is more, it is possible to transmute suffering into joy. One must face problems instead of running away from them, and the true detachment consists in being able to transform suffering into joy.

Detachment enters into relationships with people if we can love without depending on being loved. What might have been suffering because the other person does not reciprocate is transmuted into joy, because every time we are able to affirm our freedom there is a breakthrough into joy—and the breakthrough of joy in a person is never confined to that person; it spreads throughout the universe. Perhaps the secret behind this is divine grace. It is totally out of step with our rational mind or the theory of karma, of course. But perhaps the best way of seeing divine grace is to see that the miracle of life is that a catastrophe can be transformed into a victory, like the crucifixion of Christ, which turned into the coronation. From one point of view, it seemed like a catastrophe; from the divine point of view, it was a great celebration.

From our personal vantage point, there is guilt. The mind cannot possibly justify it. Reasoning will not overcome the sense of guilt; believing in a miracle is the only thing that will bring about the change, and it is an aspect of the divine perfection to be able suddenly to switch a fiasco into a victory. This is something that is totally beyond our reach. It is only by thinking of ourselves as passive with regard to the divine action that it can happen.

Psychotherapy tends to be geared to making people do something. One desperately tries to do things, like writing to the person who has been wronged, or doing good works to overcome the bad karma created by one's acts, but it is just not good enough; it will never compensate. But when we let in the greatness of the divine action, we are bringing light into darkness—into the despair of the soul. Life would be a hell if there were eternal damnation and reckoning, and life is not a hell, it is a paradise; we simply do not know it. The only way to have that realization is by giving access to the divine thinking in our thinking.

The Sufis say that if you could only have a glimpse of divine understanding, your understanding would be shattered. Guilt is tied up with our understanding, our assessment of things. This does not mean that we want to flee from guilt. Guilt, like pain, has its place. Pain gives us an awareness that we have something wrong with our physical body: perhaps we have to go to the dentist. That is the role of pain. And pain will make our hearts sincere, if it does not make us bitter. Guilt also has its purpose. It is something that we can carry as long as we are not alone in the night, as it were —as if we were carrying part of the cross of the guilt of the universe.

If we think in terms of karma, we tend to think of karma as being personal. The fact is that karma is spread out, shared. We are all part of it, and we are all part of the transmutation of the fiasco into victory. Inasmuch as one has a sense of self, then, one must think of oneself as being acted upon by the divine action rather than acting oneself.

This feeling is particularly applicable to the sense of guilt felt by many counselors who feel that they have somehow not been able really to help a patient, or, what is worse, have given a patient the wrong advice. We feel that people have been handed into our care, and then if they seem to come to grief, there is an intense feeling of guilt. Mahatma Gandhi, when he was shot, turned towards the person who shot him with his hands folded in prayer, as if to say, "Please forgive me for not having convinced you of the necessity for

nonviolence." He had a guilt feeling himself; he felt responsible. If anything, guilt is an evidence of our sense of responsibility, as part of our awareness.

The counterpart of guilt is the opposite situation, when
someone has done harm to us and we are nurturing a grievance. Many people have a festering wound in their hearts on
this account. We might be faced with this situation when a
therapist asks a patient, "Can you forgive that person?" If
the patient replies, "Oh, no, I cannot; that person has just
ruined my life, I can't forgive that person," then the only
reply we can make is, "Well, then, you will stay the way you
are. There is no way of making any progress."

There is no use in saying "I forgive" unless one really
does. This is where many people get stuck. Faced with this
stumbling block in their lives, they can never be totally
happy: one cannot dance with joy when one is nurturing this
festering wound, or a grievance against people. The feeling
of freedom that comes from the act of forgiving is a breakthrough of joy. And it is related to the feeling of guilt,
because the two are opposite poles, and they are related. If
we can forgive another person, we can forgive ourselves.

This is the only way to be free to break into further
horizons. The job of the psychotherapist is to free people;
and we can only free people if we can free ourselves. If we
are encumbered by a heavy sense of guilt, we can never free
another person. This means we must really go through the
whole process of freeing ourselves of guilt and resentment,
which means going into hell. We must be able to face all of
this, go through it and redeem ourselves or accept the divine
remission. This is the greatest gift there is—the gift of grace.
There can be no more pining after that, because if we pine,
we have not accepted the gift of grace, which is one of the
great things that is asked of the human being—to accept the
gratuitous gifts that we have not deserved.

Can our minds help us in any way? Yes, of course. We can

say, "The person who hurt me was the stick with which God hit me, so I will not blame the person." Judas had to play the role he had to play. He may have lent himself very well to that role, but that is his business. While it may not be preplanned, that is how the programming moves into place, and if we only saw what is behind it all, we would think differently. So we can release the other person from his debt to us, just as God releases us from our debt toward others; and then we will be free. It is simply a question of releasing from a debt—not holding a person in reckoning.

There is also the question of judgementalism. When I said Judas Iscariot lent himself to his role, that was a judgement of a person. Ultimately, we must discriminate between judging a situation and judging the person. We may judge a situation as being good or bad or moral or immoral or justifiable or not; judgements are relative. As far as the person is concerned, however, there should be no judgement. If we defer judgement, that makes it easier to forgive.

If we were able to get into the consciousness of the person who has harmed us and saw things from his point of view, we would understand better. For instance, Judas was very disappointed in Christ. He had been hoping that Christ would free the Holy Land from the Romans. From his point of view, Christ had violated the law of the Jews by saying he could destroy the temple, and so on. In his own mind, therefore, he was perfectly justified in what he was doing. In the same way, the person who seems to have ruined one's life may very well have justifications, whether they are right or not. We cannot enter into them. No justification is ultimate, or absolute. We may not be able to condone his action, but we could let God be the judge. Perhaps he was the one through whom God tested us so that we could become what we are supposed to become, and instead of learning from that lesson, we have just felt resentment for that person. We were totally mystified: we did not see what it was all about, and as a consequence, our progress has suffered because we keep on thinking about the person who we think has done us harm.

This is where the transcendent dimension of meditation is helpful. In the cosmic dimension, we can get into the consciousness of the other person; in the transcendent dimension, we can look upon the whole situation from a very high altitude and begin to see what is behind it. The purpose behind the programming of the universe—the objective or motivation—is not that things will run smoothly, so we can discount that possibility. The purpose is that people should progress and gain realization. In order to make that possible, people have to be tested.

There are two factors by which we can account for things: cause and purpose. The causal chain can be traced back in time, perhaps, but the purpose is like the horizon; we can never see it because as soon as we approach the horizon, we find that behind it is a still further horizon. But we can have some inkling that we are going in the right direction; we can understand that when a person seemed to be doing us harm, it was a test, so we need not blame that person anymore. When we release that person, it all becomes part of the big game of chess, and at least now we can move forward. If we can forgive him, we can forgive ourselves.

In fact, the awareness of our own guilt and responsibility can make us much more scrupulous about doing the slightest harm to people in the future. That is what can be gained from the harm that was done and that caused one's guilt, and perhaps that is the only way in which one could have learned. Something has been gained by the guilt, and what has been gained is oneself. Something has been gained in creation, and even the people against whom the act was committed have gained something because of having been put through a test. Ultimately, there is a gain in all of it, as long as one does not get stuck in despondency.

The moment we become aware, through dealing with guilt in the past, we cannot perpetuate situations that are causing undue pain. There are some situations in which pain is unavoidable, of course, and in a sense pain is not the ultimate issue, because it can be merely symptomatic of what is really wrong, just as physical pain can bring our attention to a malfunction of the body. And pain can sometimes be the price for realization; even the physical posture associated with samadhi can be excruciatingly painful to the body. The true issue is that beings should attain greater realization, and sometimes there is pain involved in this process. But we would all like to spare other people pain, and we tend to suffer more pain in ourselves than we inflict on others when we hurt them.

In the case of a divorce, there is often no way to avoid pain. The divorce itself is painful, but staying together will also cause pain. Whichever way one turns, there is still pain; the moment of confrontation can be very painful. One person discovers that the other did not love him as much as he thought, and was staying with him only out of consideration. There is a moment of extreme pain in the confrontation with truth. In general, confrontation with truth is very painful, and one would like to spare people that confrontation; but then they suffer a kind of metaphysical anguish in their soul, because it is very painful not to be sure about the truth or to be unable to rely upon the truthfulness of another person.

But, as we have said, divine grace can transform a fiasco into a victory; somehow one's relationship with a person can be handled in such a way as to make a conflict into a very beautiful sense of harmonious understanding. This is very challenging, because it means turning the tables on pain and bringing joy out of a situation that originally was very painful—like a crucifixion that turns into a resurrection.

From the personal point of view, one can't see the joy of

a painful situation. In fact, we might even say that the pain *is* the personal perspective. We can only help people over that pain by giving them the climate of joy; in that climate, their problems will look different. That is why it is not always the best solution to try to sort out a problem: sometimes the answer is in another dimension. In a game of chess, a player can try to sort out a problem and find that he is jammed; a few more moves will bring a stalemate. But in three–dimensional chess, the players can get out of the jam by moving in another dimension.

When people went to see Hazrat Inayat Khan, they expected to have to bow before this great master and then to have an opportunity to ask questions. But when they found themselves in his presence, he would just welcome them with both hands and invite them to sit next to him on the sofa, and he would speak like an old friend. They would forget all their problems, and then when they left they would often feel as if they had missed the opportunity to ask questions. Later, they would realize that they didn't have to ask the questions. The questions seemed totally superficial and unnecessary because Hazrat Inayat Khan had, by working with a higher attunement, brought them to a level of consciousness at which they were able to see into their problems themselves.

The question of guilt is a heavy one, which becomes heavier as we take on more responsibility, and it can cause us to get caught in a narrow perspective that makes it impossible for us to help other people. If we could ever realize the glory that is trying to come through in the physical planet, and the glory behind the terrible, tragic situations we encounter, we would realize how we are losing time in our tempests in our teacups when we could be participating in the cosmic celebrations in the heavens.

If we are in a state of sublime joy because we are conscious of the glory behind manifestation, then we will not depend upon the love or attachment of another person in the same way as we did before, and we may make our relationships very different by our attunement. Or we find that a humdrum job can be made beautiful because we ourselves are beautiful. It is much more important to build a world of beautiful people than to build a world of convenient gadgets, so ultimately that is where the issue is. If we can inspire a patient to be beautiful, then his problems look different, but if we try to sort his problems out with him or allow ourselves to think as he does, then it is like the blind leading the blind. That is where meditation comes in—in reaching the spiritual dimensions of counseling.

Chapter 5:

THE PERSONALITY: IMPROVING SELF-IMAGE BY DISCOVERING OUR DIVINE INHERITANCE

One of the sources of our despair and insecurity is our assessment of our own personal value. Sometimes we compare it with the value of other people, and wonder why we can't be like them. Perhaps we have a sense of what we had imagined we might become, and now find that we have not become what we had hoped to. Or perhaps our sense of values has changed, so that our idea of the ideal person has changed—and is always well ahead of what we are.

But the self-image is not the way we are; it is just the picture we make of ourselves. It is the personality that is real, that is like the territory instead of the map. Our ideal is not to be impersonal, although, as we have seen, we are both impersonal and personal in that we are both the totality and part of the totality. But it looks as though the purpose of existence is that the qualities in the totality that we call the divine perfection should become not only manifest, but even actuated in the person, so that we can say that the personality is the objective of the whole process we are in. That is why it is so important.

The role of psychology is to be the gardener of the garden of the personality—not the Pygmalion, because violence begins by the desire to make people be the way one wants them to be. We are all desperately in search of ourselves, and we do not even know what the word "ourselves" means. We have an intuition of being unique in some way, even though we know that we are really the totality that has emerged in a certain way. It is because the totality emerges in a very specific way that we are in search of our real identity. Whatever that is, we can only approximate it, but we search for it nevertheless. The curious thing is that most of what we really are, which is the totality, is not yet manifest. It does not always come through, and, in fact, sometimes the opposite comes through. What we are in reality is not yet an actuality. The words "reality" and "actuality" are not synonymous; reality is beyond time and space, and actuality is the way reality emerges in time and space. Reality is implicit, or implicate, and enfolded in our being, and in order to make it explicit, or explicate—to make it actuated—we have to be able to see those qualities in another being. That is the secret of relationship: we are always looking for ourselves in another being who is better able to manifest what we are than we ourselves have been able to do, so far. This phenomenon also shows our tremendous dependence upon other beings which means our dependence on the way those other beings appear to us.

How we see another being depends on whether we are judging him by his behavior, which is the manifestation of his being, or whether we ourselves are being in his experiential dimension. In order to reach him, we must really get into his consciousness, rather than just admire him on the strength of the way he appears.

It is the interrelationship between beings—between all beings, whether they be animals, vegetables, or even the planets or the sun, but particularly between people—that triggers off unfoldment. The beauty of our life is in the extraordinary encounter between the different parts of the totality. As Hazrat Inayat Khan said, God meets Himself in the meeting of each person with each person. This is the most sacred thing that can ever happen—like the meeting of two worlds. Even though they have the same origin, the DNA of each person has been narrowed down in the course of time, so that although the universe is in each one of them, it is becoming more unique in its way. Not only the encounter of but the maintaining of the relationship between two people is the very impetus that triggers off transformation in our being.

We are able to communicate with people all the time, and not necessarily only by talking with them; we must be able to carry beings in our souls or our hearts. Hazrat Inayat Khan once said that from the time you smile upon a person, you have established a mutual responsibility; that person becomes part of your being, and you become part of his being. There is an osmosis taking place. The great moment is when one discovers oneself in another being, or discovers certain aspects of one's being in another being. The other being need not even be human; we can discover ourselves as beings of light when we watch a glorious sunrise. We can feel, "This is what I really am; I'm a being of light. This is my true home." We discover one aspect of ourselves just by watching the sunrise. Every time we look upon a person and see in him something that is familiar because it is really our own self that we are discovering through him, there is a moment of glory. It is an experience that strengthens our faith in that which we did not believe was possible, because it was just too beautiful; and it takes away our fear about inadequacy.

Inadequacy is caused by identifying with our own self-image, and getting caught up in it, restricted in it, and sclerosed in it. We all tend to feel that we are not perfect, so we are always posed with the problem of how to undergo transformation, how to improve. One has to work continually with perfecting oneself, just as an artist might work continually on a work of art to keep improving it. The trouble with the personality, however, is that we cannot transform it by our will, however much we might wish to; and yet we know that the greatness of human beings consists in mastery, the ability to monitor and to pilot their lives, to be "in the saddle." Transforming the personality is more subtle than this implies; it resembles biofeedback more than it does the outward work of the artist.

Many functions of the body are purely autonomic: they are under the control of the autonomic nervous system, and there is no way of acting directly on muscles that are under its control except by a "bias"—for example, by using imagination. Images will somehow re-set the whole balance of the autonomic nervous system. The same is true at the level of the personality. A person might work at it as much as he liked, saying, "I am strong, I am strong, I am strong"; but when faced with his boss, he might still find himself rather shaky. The process does not work, which is why so many people feel so desperate. When people feel they have really done all they can to make themselves feel more self-confident and then lose their confidence when it comes to the point, it can only add to their feelings of inadequacy. But there is a way of enlisting a power beyond one's personal power or personal will. The will is in some way connected with the consciousness, so if we can change the setting of our consciousness, we will by the same token change the setting of our will.

The methods I prescribe for working with the personality include, first of all, working with the cosmic dimension of consciousness. If we extend our consciousness into the consciousness of all beings, we can experience what we look like to people, and what people look like to themselves; we begin to communicate with all beings, including animals and plants, and we loosen thereby the boundaries of the self-image and begin to merge with the beings of all beings. This is the first step—to establish communication—and it is particularly important for people who feel inadequate, because people who feel inadequate are generally extremely self-conscious, which means they have confined their consciousness to their notion of themselves and are unable to communicate with other people.

I remember meeting a young girl who was very shy and who felt she was always left out of conversations because she did not know how to relate to other people; she didn't know how to start a conversation with people because she didn't know what to say. I said, "Well, actually the conversations between people are on the whole rather stupid, so you don't have to try to be brilliant. The reason why people converse is not to say brilliant things, it's just to communicate. Even if you talk nonsense, it doesn't matter, as long as you really start communicating. You start by talking unintelligently, but eventually you will improve; occasionally you'll say a few things that are kind of witty, and then you'll be okay." This point of view made a great deal of difference to her. We find the same phenomenon when two strangers encounter one another in an elevator: that moment can be embarrassing unless one of them says something. Most of the things that we say are not particularly brilliant, but that does not matter; the point is only to establish communication.

We have said that we will always try to look at things from two different angles. Up to this point, we have approached the problem of working with the personality from the personal point of view. Now we shall look at it from the divine point of view. This means looking at ourselves as being the totality that emerges. So long as we think of ourselves as wanting to perfect ourselves, it will not work; but as soon as we are able to experience the vastness of our being, and, what is more, experience ourselves as passive with regard to the divine perfection rather than actively trying to improve ourselves, then things begin to happen: the whole attitude changes.

We can begin by working with certain specific qualities. One quality that tends to be absent in a person who feels inadequate is power. A person may feel unable to deal with big issues and so would prefer escaping them to facing them; he may be afraid of facing strong people, or worry that his appearance or what he says is not inspiring; and he may, in fact, develop an aversion towards himself. I have said earlier that there is a relationship between the self-image and the image we make of the universe. The way to experience power in oneself is to experience the power that moves the universe.

Instead of looking at things from our own angle, we must get into the consciousness of the universe and experience all the power that is unfurled in the motion of the stars and the atoms and the sap in the trees and all the life force that we express ourselves—of which even our bodies are an expression—the power that is continually moving forward and breaking into new horizons. I have said that the cosmic dimension has to do with space in the sense that one is not confined to one's location in space, but consciousness extends into the vastness of space; but it is also the vastness of understanding and the vastness of power, the vastness of compassion and the vastness of love—the vastness of everything one could conceive of. It is, in fact, what we mean by divine compassion.

We have described the experience of lying on the grass feeling the merging of one's body with the fabric of the universe, as if the borderline had disappeared altogether. The same thing can be done with the power that is moving the universe: we can experience ourselves as being part of that power. It has to do with the sense of vastness, and the best thing about it is that in that state, one is free from the tyranny of the ego. Many people have lost their ability to experience themselves as the totality. That ability is found in some of the people who live closer to nature, like Native Americans, Africans, and many Indians. It is possible to feel oneself so much part of the totality that the frontier between oneself and the totality has petered out, and the immediate result of this is a sense of vastness. The frontiers of one's being are extended until there are no frontiers anymore.

The search for power is problematic, because many people have suffered from the abuse of power and so have misgivings about it. Many people do not want to develop personal power, and, therefore, do not know how to deal with people who have strong egos. The question is how to develop the quality of power without developing a powerful ego—without inflicting one's power on others. This is where we have to refer to the transcendent dimension and the concept of God: we have to be the instruments through which comes a power beyond our power.

In discussing biofeedback, I said that one cannot apply his will in some cases; but there is a way of galvanizing a will beyond the personal will to take over from the personal will and act upon the system. The key to this is the ability to coordinate a sense of perfection with a sense of precariousness—the divine perfection suffering in human limitation. Just as one can be aware of being the whole and also part of the whole, or both transient and eternal, one can be the precarious instrument of a power that is overwhelming without affirming one's own power, and also identify with the divine power. This is all beyond logic.

To arrive at the transcendent dimension, we must become aware of our divine inheritance and discover all the different elements that have come into the formation of our being— all the richness that has come into our being. When we talked about the transcendent dimension, we said that in it we discover our eternity—we discover that we have always been and will always be a certain aspect of our being. This is what we must do to discover our divine inheritance. We can do this by disidentifying ourselves with everything that is transient in us: our bodies, our minds, our personalities, even our consciousness. We can think of ourselves as visitors from outer space who are visiting the planet and experiencing conditions on the planet, and have therefore borrowed bodies made out of the fabric of the planet and minds made out of the thinking of people on the planet; and we have borrowed qualities from our ancestors. These are all things that are borrowed, and therefore transient. When we disidentify ourselves with them, we can have a grasp of our real being behind all those masks—all those layers that have been added in the course of the descent.

There comes a time when one is able to say, "I am the divine power"—not just "I am the instrument of the divine power," but, "I am the divine power. I am the divine truth. I am the divine insight into all things. That is my true being. And I have allowed myself to be caught in a perspective in which I thought I was 'that person.' Now I have discovered what I really am." That is what we call awakening from a perspective.

How do you proceed if you are the psychotherapist? There is no use in telling another person to attain to this state of awakening if you cannot do it yourself, because that person is looking for himself in you. It is true that one is taught in psychoanalysis not to be in any way a prototype, so that the patient can transfer to one. But in fact, the way that people progress in life is by seeing themselves in a person whom they idealize as being the model of what they would like to be. In order to help a person who is very insecure to have confidence in his being you must yourself be aware of being the divine power. This means you must overcome your personal power, or your personal conscious-ness, and get into your higher consciousness. This requires, on the one hand, sinking your personal consciousness and, on the other hand, awakening an impersonal consciousness. That is the secret of samadhi.

In therapy, many people promote relaxation. This can simply lead to a trance state, and, in any case, relaxation on its own is not good enough. It must be accompanied by a heightened awareness—but a totally impersonal awareness. This is true even in relaxing the body: the best way to relax the body is to know how to contract and then relax the muscles, and then find a tone in them. The muscles must not flop: there must be a harmonious tone in them. When we go to sleep, we let go of the physical environment so that the impressions from the senses do not reach the brain anymore. Then we let go of our control of our thoughts, and as a consequence our thoughts begin to wander at random, or in a manner that seems random, in a state of reverie; and we no longer pay attention to them. The emotions must also shift from joy or sorrow to peace. While this is happening, there is a change in consciousness: consciousness is *awaken-ing* in sleep from the personal vantage point. If one were aware of the change that takes place when one is going to sleep, one would realize that there is a change, first of all, in one's notion of the physical world—one experiences that which transpires behind that which appears. One is no longer caught in the data of the senses, but is beginning to grasp the reality behind that which manifests in time and space. But this is where consciousness generally blanks out: there is no memory of that awareness normally when one gets back into ordinary consciousness.

The other thing that happens in sleep is that one's notion of oneself is totally changed. Most of us remember some of our dreams, but can we remember what it felt like to be dreaming? How the universe felt? We may remember impressions or images, but do we remember the feeling of our relationship with the universe? And do we remember our notion of ourselves? If we can remember, we will realize that our notion of ourselves was totally modified—we were different people. The difference is that we were universal. We were much less like the person we thought we were, a definite and limited person. We had many more qualities and were much less defined. In fact, we discovered ourselves as being the nameless and the formless and the spaceless and the timeless—another dimension of our being altogether. Ordinary consciousness cannot encompass this vastness. That is why ordinary consciousness generally blanks out altogether and there is a break in consciousness, so that we do not remember what it was like when we get back into our ordinary consciousness.

If we can accept the vastness of our being and accept that we are different from what we thought we were, we will be able to encompass this vastness as we awaken in sleep. The best way to do this is to look back upon the way we saw things and realize that we were caught in a perspective. Then we have the feeling that we have awakened from that perspective, and we will have intense, but impersonal, awareness—because we are not caught by the notion of the personal self, as we used to be. The secret is to realize that we are the nameless and the formless, treading beyond the walks of men into a no man's land without path and without azimuth, and beyond time and space. We are where all things originate, and we are all those things that have not yet manifested—the non-manifest and the not-yet-manifested.

Then we can look on the physical plane from a new perspective, or, better still, we can look on the perspective with which we looked on the physical world and realize that it was just *a* perspective—that things appeared as they did because we were caught in a perspective. In fact, we must be passive instead of active if we are going to follow the Sufi method, which is to be passive towards the divine thinking. We are "thought of"; we exist as being "thought of." And our being is an act of glory—a many-splendored reality.

After we have experienced this dimension, when we try to get back into our personalities there is a feeling of having to constrict ourselves to be able to fit into that narrow mold, and there is a desire to burst the seams of that mold so that we are able to bring more of our being into that narrow capacity. We experience an elasticity of our personality that is able to expand, so that more and more of the richness of our being comes through.

Chapter 6:

AWAKENING

The only thing that stands in the way of expressing the divine power is in the mind, in the assumption that one is the personality that one thought one was. This problem is analogous to that of a person whose father has put a fortune in the bank for him but who does not know about it and so thinks he is poor. Limitation, which exists only in the mind, is caused by lack of awareness.

The method we adopted to overcome this limitation was, on the one hand, sinking or diminishing the activity of those parts of our being that are transient, like the body and the mind. We let go of the body and let the mind drift, or "space out." The personality—the sense of one's identity—was scattered. There was no boundary to ourselves anymore. On the other hand, there was an enhancing of awareness, but a purely impersonal awareness. We were able to look down upon our personalities—not in the geographical sense, but from a perspective that enabled us to look upon the personal aspect of ourselves objectively. As long as we identify with the personal aspect, we cannot change it, but if we can look at it objectively and see that it is a construction of the mind, then the whole construction breaks down. One does not have to do anything about it; it just breaks down.

We can then develop the quality of insight, which is one of the secrets to developing intuition. If we are centered in our personal consciousness, there is a tendency to think, "Well, I know this, and this I don't know. To know it, I would have to have some evidence through my senses, or I would have to understand it with my mind." That is the limitation in which we find ourselves when we are in our personal consciousness.

We have already noted that when we are in the cosmic dimension, we can get into the consciousness of all beings. For instance, we could think of a person who is very close to us and then try to get into that person's consciousness and experience what it is like to be that person. We may experience that person's misgivings, fears, hopes, aspirations, and idiosyncracies, or whether he or she has a great deal of temperament or is cautious, or affable, or "uptight," or conventional, or permissive. We can experience many qualities in that person: whether he or she is loving or not so loving, compassionate or not so compassionate—not as *we* judge him but as the person judges himself, because when we enter his consciousness we are not really entering into his personality, but into his image of his personality.

If you are a therapist who is counseling patients and you get into their consciousness, to start with you only get into the consciousness of their self-images—their representations of themselves. This might, to some extent, tally with the personality, but does not altogether.

In his ordinary consciousness, a person is only aware of a very small fraction of his being, so we cannot say that we realy are getting into his total experience just by transferring into his consciousness. Furthermore, there is a whole area of thoughts that one does not admit to oneself—or at least does not want others to pry into. That area is out of bounds: we must not try in any way to unlock the secrets of the heart of a person if he does not wish us to, simply to satisfy our curiosity. This may be done only with someone who is so close to us that he is prepared to let us look not only into his soul, but also into his thoughts. But if we really want to get into the being of a person from the inside, we must experience what he would be experiencing if he were in his higher consciousness—in other words, if he were in the consciousness we described as necessary for discovering our divine inheritance. We have to experience what that person could be if he would be what he should be, which, in fact, is the divine consciousness in that person. We might say that the personal consciousness is the divine consciousness, but it is also a consciousness that has been isolated in some sense —cut away and alienated from the total consciousness, although it never completely loses the connection.

This is where the cosmic dimension must be supplemented by the transcendent. The Sufi Ibn al-'Arabi says that we have to get into the consciousness of the nonmanifest— all the potentials that are not yet manifest in a person. It would be a little bit like experiencing the root of a sprout; all that we see is the little sprout that grows above the surface of the earth, but if we could get into the root and see that, too, we could see all the possibilities that are there but have not come through yet—like the eggs inside a chicken that are not ready to be laid, but are still on their way. In the person, there are many qualities that are on their way, that are not manifest; and that is the only way to understand a person. Most often, the person himself is unaware of all those qualities, but by seeing them we help him see them in himself; we can act like a midwife who is bringing these qualities into actuation.

We do this by getting into the transcendent dimension of consciousness together with the cosmic. We get into the cosmic dimension by overcoming the idea of being located in space—by extending consciousness and reaching out into the consciousness of the universe, of all beings. The best way to do it is to be able to look upon ourselves from outside ourselves; for instance, we might ask how our face would look from the vantage point of that other person. And there is a sense of vastness. At this point, we have to supplement this dimension of consciousness with the transcendent dimension, which we do by objectivizing the body and the mind, awakening from identification with that which is transient, and discovering our eternity. Once we have done that in ourselves, now we must carry the same thing further so that we are not doing it just to ourselves. We must grasp the reality behind the world of actuality—the many-splendored reality that is coming through in the forms of the flowers, the species of insects, the animals, and humans, coming through in the events. In fact, we get into the programming behind the universe, or the thinking behind the universe. Then we find how joyous, inventive, and spontaneous that programming is—tingling with ideas, trying out all kinds of new ideas all the time: testing them out, picking up the feedback, and reprogramming itself according to the feedback. And not only reprogramming itself, but even projecting the hardware that is necessary to implement the feedback. It is like seeing from the angle opposite to the angle from which one usually sees things. One generally experiences the result of the whole process, and is caught in that perspective. When we reverse our perspective, we see from inside, as if we were looking into the DNA of the cells of the body and the patterning of the brain, entering into the way of thinking of the enzymes and then understanding the body from that angle, rather than observing it by cutting up a corpse, for example.

What is truly amazing is that we find that the programming is all moving toward a purpose. If we analyze things, we discover, perhaps, something about the cause, but never the purpose—the direction in which it is moving and the motivation behind it, what it is aiming at. And the purpose is not a concrete thing that can be defined, but is constantly breaking into new horizons and improving all the time. There is more and more, and better and better, organization. There is more interaction between the parts to enable intelligence to come through. The DNA of the universe is the thinking that is coded into the structures of the amino acids, like the thinking that has come through in the notes of music of the toccatas and fugues of Bach. And though it is inventive, creative, spontaneous, and exploratory, it has become "homonized" in the course of evolution, in the word of Teilhard de Chardin. It has become human; it has led towards the miracle that God has become human. The whole process of the universe, at least on the planet Earth, has become homonized, which means that it has become us.

Now the purpose of life begins to come through a little more clearly: all of this marvel of creation has come through in a being and that being is us. And still it continues to strive to improve its functioning and its ability to bring all the richness of creation through. Here we are, struggling with our inadequacies, when we realize that we *are* the many-splendored reality that is trying to come through, and that we are standing in the way of its coming through because of our self-image. That is the breakthrough, the peak experience: the moment when we are able to look upon the whole process from "outer space," with a tremendous perspective of the whole meaningfulness of life. That is the only time that our lives, or the lives of other people, make sense.

It is true that when we are in our personal consciousness, we may experience an awareness coming through us, as if we were "the eyes through which God sees," as the Sufis say. But that is only one side of the story; the other side is the realization that "I am the divine awareness. I am the divine glance." This is awakening: to realize, "I am the divine glance. I cast the light of consciousness upon all things and reveal their secrets, because I am the very thinking that I watch manifest in objects. I am that thinking that has become those objects." This is a very far cry from sitting in the psychoanalyst's study and getting caught up in all the inhibitions of the patient. What the therapist should do instead is teach the patient to look upon himself objectively instead of identifying with his personal self, then accepting himself; because we are the totality and also part of the totality, the divine consciousness and also the instrument of the divine consciousness, the divine power and the instrument of the divine power—both at the same time. And what is gained by this is that the totality does come through in our being.

The only way we can realize this is by overcoming our fundamental metaphysics, which are: me here, God up there; God-other-than-me, the-universe-other-than-me— "me" being our personality or our body or our understanding. Once we have overcome all the metaphysical assumptions we had in the past, we can come to the same realization about love, compassion, and ecstasy—realize that "I am the emotion that moves the universe; I am the wine of the divine sacrament, and all are moved into existence by my ecstasy." Ecstasy is the most creative of all energies, and when we are in the cosmic consciousness, we can get into the ecstasy of the universe, because behind the thinking of the universe there is an emotion. Behind a toccata and fugue, there is not just thinking, there is an emotion. If we look into the stars—if we get into the motion of the stars, rather than just thinking of them as little lights in the dark sky—we will be overwhelmed by the ecstasy of the choreography of the heavens. We can get into the emotion of the sun as it rises over the horizon—the same sun that looks so magnificent when we are watching it in our own consciousness. What about the emotion of the sun? In fact, the sun is picking up our emotion as we experience him.

We can get into the motion of the birds singing, the deer in the forest, the falcon on the wing, the flowers turning toward the light—and the broken heart of God suffering from the limitation of the human condition, and the joy of release and of resurrection. We can get into the human drama that is enacted every day in every little nook of the planet—the vastness of emotion. Then we see how insignificant our little emotions are, and how we are missing the whole show, to which we have been invited, because we are so caught up in our little emotions.

When we flow with all this emotion, we are part of it, and when we realize that we are the divine emotion, it transforms our whole being. If we try to develop more compassion, or more control of our temper, we cannot do it, because the personal will rests on a fallacy—the personal consciousness, which is, at least, a relative fallacy, because although there is focalized consciousness, it is only a condition of consciousness, not a "thing." We tend to reify consciousness, but consciousness is not a thing in its own right, it is only a condition. When we get into the experience of the will of the universe, then miracles happen that could never occur through the enforcing of our own will. That is the secret of bringing about transformation: triggering off the will of the universe instead of interfering with our own will. It is also the secret of biofeedback—promoting change by getting the mind and the will out of the way.

This is the change people find in themselves after a retreat; they come out of a retreat and think, "Look at all these people—they're like puppets caught by invisible threads, pulled, rushing about without knowing really what they're rushing about for, caught up in their opinions and their emotions and their sense of values. And they can't see the wood for the trees, And I was in exactly the same place all this time, but now, somehow, I've awakened from it; now I can see the whole 'trip' so clearly." It is when we experience that awakening that we have a strength that makes us feel we could move the universe. The word "impossible" does not exist. And we can see every person according to his emotion—just where he stands according to his emotion and his realization. We can see that one person is looking for vulgar emotions, while another is looking for sublime emotions; one person is looking for personal satisfaction, while another can only live when he is living for something that is more meaningful than his own personal purpose. We can see this because we are allowing the divine insight to work instead of our personal insight. What is more, when we are able to see into a person, we help him see into himself. Otherwise, we cannot help him; we can only help him see where he is by means of a confrontation with himself. We cannot advise people what to do, but we can make them see something they had not seen before.

Of course, there is some relationship between this insight and one's motivation. If one is motivated by personal gain or by wanting to manipulate others, one will never have this insight. That is where detachment comes in, and that is why this is the path of the sannyasin, the hermit who is detached as far as his own interest is concerned. This is the person who can still be involved with people as long as he is not pursuing a personal purpose; and, therefore, he must be free in himself.

If we are free in ourselves, we can free others. If we are binding other people to ourselves, then we are not ourselves free, and we cannot free others. The goal of the therapist is to free people—from their points of view, their personal emotions, their fears, and even from their personal volition, if they so wish—but only if they wish to reach beyond themselves.

Chapter 7:

RELATIONSHIP

To see how the principles we have been discussing thus far work in practice, we can examine a case history.

John loves Cynthia, or has been living in a loving relationship with her for eight years; perhaps they are married. Suddenly, Elizabeth comes on the scene. John falls in love with Elizabeth, and so a problem arises. The people involved in a drama of this sort are in a bind—possibly even a double or triple bind. Each one of them might be sitting in his or her own little room and trying to figure it out: "What am I going to do?"

John has to decide whether he really wants to be with Elizabeth or whether his relationship with her is just a passing affair and he should stay with Cynthia; or perhaps he does not wish to disturb his marriage. There may be more than two alternatives, but for the sake of simplicity, we can consider only two: either he stays with Cynthia or goes with Elizabeth. Perhaps at one moment he is convinced he should leave Cynthia and be with Elizabeth, but then feels unhappy because there is an aspect he left out of account. So he looks at the whole situation again, and then becomes convinced he should be with Cynthia and should abandon Elizabeth. Or he may ask himself whether there is not some way to compromise, decides that there is not, and has to begin all over again to make a definite decision. He is, in short, dithering —something we all do at some time.

The secret of his predicament is focusing. When we look at a problem, there are many things implicated in it, so we tend to bring into focus only a few aspects of the problem at a time. Because we cannot normally bring the entire problem into focus, we see only a few aspects of it at a time, while the rest of it falls out of focus, much as our memory of a person may include a few features of his face or the sound of his voice while leaving vague innumerable other aspects of his being. When we realize that there are some aspects of the problem that are out of focus, as soon as we do focus on them the aspects we were considering earlier fall out of focus.

In a situation like the one in our case study, one or more of the people involved may, in desperation, seek the help of a therapist—and God help the therapist who gives them advice. It is difficult enough for the people involved, and a therapist can only make it more difficult for them by giving his or her opinion, since the therapist cannot possibly know all the circumstances. We have said that, optimally, we should be able to use intuition, but nevertheless it is most important for the people in search of answers to make their own decisions. Given all these factors, what is there a therapist can do when people come, in desperation, for help?

Let us begin by bringing a few aspects of the problem into focus. In the beginning, John had fallen in love with Cynthia. In her, he found something very meaningful to him —in fact, she probably helped him to find himself. He may have seen in her qualities that were the same as his, or qualities that challenged his; there may have been either an affinity or a complementarity, but in one way or another there was an action of Cynthia upon John that was transforming. When they came to know each other better, he found things in her he did not like, and she found things in him she did not like. They may have had different habits or attitudes that necessitated giving in on one side or the other. In some cases, it is always one partner who gives in while the other has his way—which is soul-killing—while in others the partners take turns giving in. In either case, there is some dissatisfaction, but both partners usually realize that they must give up something in order to make a relationship work.

At first, when he was in love with her, John had seen Cynthia in her real being. When he got closer to her, he began to see her personality, and at that point he may have lost sight of her real being; he may have been convinced that he had seen wrongly and that her real being was in fact the personality he later began to discover. Now, her personality is masking her real being from him. He thinks he must have made a mistake when he first fell in love with her, when in fact it is the other way around: he had seen her originally the way she is, and now is judging her by the way in which her real being comes through in her personality. Because of this, he is forcing her into herself—into the image he makes of her. In the end, his impact upon her makes her lose confidence in her real being, and she begins to identify with the being that he thinks she is. It is very difficult to fight against the social impact of the environment upon one's assessment of oneself.

If John were in his higher consciousness, he would keep on seeing Cynthia the way he saw her in the beginning, which is to say in her real being, and he would not allow his judgement about her to take away his faith in what she really is. He would, therefore, help her to become her real being. By denigrating her, he draws her lower down, or further and further away from her real being; and then he is dissatisifed with her, so he destroys her, simply by his lack of loyalty to her soul.

In the meantime, of course, both people have changed considerably. They may once have had wonderful exchanges of feeling and emotions, thoughts, ideals, motivations, and purposes; now they are out of sync—they cannot relate to one another. Their relationship has become a humdrum affair, a routine taken for granted, and they feel the weight of being bound to one another—of not being free.

Under these circumstances, John meets Elizabeth. In her, he sees all that he has idealized, and forgets that he had seen it in Cynthia. He begins to feel that his relationship with Cynthia is holding him back from a vital necessity, because he feels he can only unfold his being by being in contact with Elizabeth. She reciprocates, and it is always flattering to be loved; perhaps she herself sees things in John that are meaningful to her. In fact, they may feel that they are meant for each other and that the previous relationship was simply a mistake. John, however, may now hesitate; for one thing, he sees that he is causing Cynthia pain, and for another he feels that he is failing to fulfill his pledge of loyalty to her, to stand by her in all circumstances. If she reacts angrily, he may find her still less lovable, even if he is aware that her anger stems from her sense of betrayal.

Cynthia's position is especially difficult. She does not wish John to stay with her unless he really wants to, but she has spent years with him and now cannot face a new life without him. In any case, she loves John and feels she has been demoted and displaced. In some cases, she may understand that John needs this contact with a person who is meaningful to him, and will have enough breadth of vision or tolerance to allow it to go on as long as it does not go too far—a measure that differs significantly from one person to another. This does not necessarily relieve her suffering, however, and the time may come when she, too, is torn; she may feel that being too tolerant is not getting anyone anywhere, that all three are suffering and that perhaps she is out of place and should leave. If there are children, they may complicate her feelings still more by making it more difficult to leave.

Elizabeth does not really want to hurt Cynthia, but she may feel that after all, John was never really happy with Cynthia and that it is his happiness that is at stake. When two people find each other, it is of utmost importance for them to be able to be together, and she finds it terrible that he cannot find his way to her because he is bound to another.

This is a typical situation, and we can see that behind it is a need to unfold oneself in contact with another person. The people involved may not themselves realize this, but we can look upon it as one of the primary forces behind the drama. I would not be so foolhardy as to offer a solution to a problem like this one. The therapist takes on a great responsibility if he or she promotes a confrontation. John may not wish to admit to Cynthia how meaningful Elizabeth is to him; he may want to preserve her feelings—he may even fear that she will commit suicide, as sometimes happens— and so he may want to avoid making her face the truth. She may be suffering because she doesn't know whether he really loves her at all anymore, or whether his attraction to Elizabeth is only a passing phase, so that her opting out would only destroy a relationship that is still very meaningful to her. If the therapist brings about a confrontation, which is what many marriage counselors do, he or she is precipitating the situation, which may lead to a very sudden change. In some cases, when the situation continues to stagnate, it can become like an abscess that must be pricked in order for healing to begin; and if the people involved do not have the courage to face each other, the therapist may be instrumental in bringing about their confrontation.

On the other hand, sometimes the persons involved do not confront themselves, and this becomes an issue of greater importance. Without necessarily trying to bring them together, the therapist may persuade them to confront themselves; but only if the therapist can keep the secret of their hearts is he or she allowed to sit there and receive their confessions. Confessions cannot be forced, but a person in a quandary may feel a very great need to open up his heart; if he is not facing himself, he may be able to do so by verbalizing about the situation.

A priori, that person is caught in his personal consciousness and is not aware of the forces behind the situation. If he were in a higher state of consciousness, he would have a totally different view of the situation. He has been caught up in the focusing process we described earlier and is unable to see clearly. The only way in which he would be able to see more clearly would be to have a vast, panoramic view, so that he could understand what other issues lay behind the question at hand.

We might note parenthetically that this can pose even more difficulties; often, those of us in spiritual movements come across people who say that their partners are not in favor of the spiritual life and that their own spirits are dampened by this; they find that the attunement of their being is continually being arrested by having to deal with someone who is denigrating their spiritual quest. In marriages and even in friendships, we often find that the egos of people tend to wallow in denigrating another person, which gives them a sense of ascendancy but which may ultimately destroy the other person by continually making him lose confidence in himself, and then that person wants to get out of the relationship he now finds so soul-killing.

But then the partner, who was denigrating him, may be in a terrible state of desolation if he leaves, so the situation can prove to be quite cruel.

Returning to the problem of the triangle, we find that from the vantage point of the cosmic consciousness and the transcendent consciousness it looks quite different. Even if a person feels he cannot evolve spiritually in that confining atmosphere, he may realize that it is in fact a challenge to his spiritual unfoldment, and that the more he is challenged the more he will be able to develop. Just as in learning to play the piano or type or drive, the best way to increase one's capacity is to challenge oneself into more and more difficult situations. It may be that a person who was over-stressed by a situation because he is not working with his spiritual awareness finds that when he does work with his spiritual awareness, the very person who was challenging him or trying to denigrate him no longer has a handle on him. The usual argument used to denigrate a person who is spiritually inclined or very idealistic is to accuse him of not having his feet on the ground. But, in fact, if one is in a very high state of consciousness, one is somehow unflappable, and people cannot affect one; their denigration simply fails to stick. This is the place of detachment in spirituality. One can be extremely involved with a person in the sense of caring for him or loving him, but can be detached in the sense that that person cannot take away one's attunement or consciousness. Then the whole relationship changes. The person may not be able to stand the fact that he or she cannot reach one, and may become angry, but if he finds that his anger gets no response—that he has been unable to arouse one's own anger by his—he finds that his manipulations simply do not work. He finds the object of his denigration is in an area he cannot reach.

In the case of John, Cynthia, and Elizabeth, we find that if he is not facing the issue with Cynthia and trying to start fresh with Elizabeth, the same problems he had with Cynthia are going to arise with Elizabeth, because he has not really solved them. All three partners are caught in their personal consciousness. The solution lies at another level: seeing where the problems are and how the people involved can transform themselves in order to be able to meet the problems. Changing the outside may not be necessary, and is not always going to change the inside.

However, it may very well be possible that there must be a change in the outside situation. If John and Elizabeth are in fact a perfect match, it seems tragic that something as beautiful as the gift of love cannot become a reality. Failing to try to make the ideal an actuality can be like refusing a beautiful gift.

There is no standard solution to a problem like this, but what is certain is that looking at it from the personal point of view makes it impossible to see clearly into it. Perhaps one of the parties must take a stand if the others do not: for example, Cynthia may have to take things in hand and either leave or force John to make a choice—to confront the situation he was trying to evade. This may compel him, if he is capable of it, to look at things from a higher angle and realize that perhaps after all he did not give the chance he should have given to his relationship with Cynthia, which was why he was looking elsewhere, and that perhaps he would not have found what he was looking for in Elizabeth even though it looked as if he might at the time. The therapist's only way of helping them is to get them to get into a very high state of consciousness and see the whole thing: the meaning of their lives and what life is doing to them in terms of their unfoldment. They can be helped to realize that situations on the earth will never be perfect—in fact, are sometimes really disastrous—but that they can handle things beautifully. That is how we can bring about heaven on earth: by handling ugly things beautifully.

Chapter 8:

TO BECOME WHAT I AM

I sometimes encounter a person who finds it difficult to rise out of a limited perspective—who feels that some part of himself does not want to transcend or go beyond the old images, so that he finds himself involved in an intense inner struggle. This is because when one is exposed to something that is uplifting and inspiring, whether it be a person, a piece of music, or a situation, the experience unleashes forces that aspire towards one's ideal and give one the strength to overcome what is called in the East "the temptation of the world."

As long as there is a need to find fulfillment or satisfaction in what worldly situations offer, it is probably best that one should pursue the fulfillment of that need to one's satisfaction—providing one does not altogether close the door to one's higher purpose. A group of Buddhist monks from Ceylon who were visiting Paris were observed spending most of their time in the nightclubs, and we can only conclude from this that it would have been better if they had lived a married life—or even a wild life—and then become monks, rather than the other way around. It is possible to overstress oneself in following the spiritual path if one is not up to it; some people even develop an aversion to the spitirual way, or find themselves torn because they feel the spiritual path is keeping them from the fulfillment they need in their personal satisfaction. This, of course, depends on which path one is taking. The teaching of Hazrat Inayat Khan in this respect is not to be desireless, but to look upon desire as an expression of the divine impulse towards manifestation: to be continually balanced between enthusiasm and detachment. Enthusiasm makes things happen, while detachment frees one from involvement and makes it possible not to depend on the results of one's efforts—to go on beating one's own records rather than resting on one's laurels. Hazrat Inayat Khan taught that there is a great strength to be gained by fulfilling an impulse—for example, the desire to build a house or to play music—because one has put one's desire into action. Following the spiritual path does not rule out improving one's worldly condition.

On the other hand, detachment gives a still greater power, which comes through at those moments when one is, for example, giving up a pursuit that was rewarding for something that is, perhaps, greater in itself but less rewarding. I once met a young man who thought he wanted to be an author but felt he was unable to write a book. He had tried writing books, but neither he nor anyone else liked them, and since he saw no other purpose in life than being an author, he wanted to commit suicide. I asked him if there were anything else he wanted to do, but he insisted there was not. I told him, "Okay, I promise you will be an author, but in the meantime you should become something else— pursue some other line, like a hobby." He said he had been a photographer but that photography did not interest him very much; I told him, "Become a photographer, and when you become successful, give up photography and become an author." Although he expressed some doubt about becoming an author by becoming a photographer, he took my advice and became a successful photographer. Years later, he came to me and told me he had earned a great deal of money as a photographer, but, although he found it difficult to do so, he had given up photography to become an author—and had published a book. This was a case of detachment—giving something up in order to progress.

Both detachment and achievement give people a sense of power, so there is a choice between the two. The pursuit of personal satisfaction in the world has its part to play, and if a person feels he is sacrificing something that is important to him because of his spiritual quest, he probably should not make that sacrifice. When he attributes less value to the pursuit of worldly things and begins to realize the value of spiritual goals, his attractions to the world will fall away naturally, and there will be no sacrifice. The person who feels unable to transcend the personal perspective is often feeling guilty about not giving vent to his spiritual ideals—a not-uncommon problem. It is at a time like this in one's development that an encounter with a spiritually enlightened being might bring about the change one needs. There is a tendency to get into a rut; one is always busy, and yet one constantly feels a sense of sacrificing something very important eating into one's heart and soul. We are always sacrificing the more important for the more urgent in life. And if that is the case, we must do something about it.

One might decide to take a trip to India, and, in fact, many people do go to India on a "guru hunt." They most often come back disappointed because the truly great masters retire higher into the mountains, or deeper into the jungle, if they are found. So many people are disappointed. But it is still true that, in the effort to make one's spiritual ideal a reality, the strongest impact is that of coming in contact with a being who is highly realized. We may entertain ideas about masters in the Himalayas, but if we can discover a master, then we realize that our ideal is a reality. But what is far more important is to become that reality oneself, rather than settle for visiting a high being.

When I was a young man, I went on a "guru hunt" in the Himalayas, and walked three days in the snow and ice, catching pneumonia, to find a rishi in a cave. When I did find him, he signaled me not to come in, so I sat in the snow meditating. When I opened my eyes, he was smiling at me. He said, "Why have you come so far to see what you should be?" The answer was that in order to become what I am, I have to see myself in another.

The method I recommend defies all the conventional ideas of having a picture of one's guru in front of one—the sort of personal attachment to the personal guru that can be very restrictive and turn into idolatry. Jelal ad-din Rumi, a Sufi poet, said that the murshid, or teacher, is the destroyer of the idol that the pupil makes of him. So what I advocate is to represent to oneself an ideal being. One imagines going on a pilgrimage and coming across the most marvelous being one could ever imagine—the being one has always dreamt of. One sits in his or her presence; at first one is just over-whelmed, but then one begins to make a very clear represen-tation of this being: whether it is a man or woman, old or young, bearded or beardless. This representation is not only of the being's physical appearance, but also of the kind of magnetism radiating from that being, the light in his eyes, his aura, the kind of penetrating glance that being has, and the sense of his or her mastery, compassion, love, suffering, joy, peace, truth—all the qualities of that being. Because every time one earmarks a quality, one experiences it one-self. When one thinks of the light in that being, one feels luminous; when one thinks of the mastery in that being, it gives one a sense of mastery oneself; when one thinks of that being's magnetism, one feels the magnetism of one's own being. One reacts to the impact of that being upon one; if one is able to make that being real to oneself and can imagine him and represent him as real, one will undergo the impact. And then one finds that one does not have to sit in the presence of that being anymore, because one has discovered him in oneself. Wherever one goes, one will be that being.

The secret behind this is that one would never be able to represent this being to oneself if it were not one's own real being. We would prefer just to project an ideal being, because we do not have the courage to be what we are; we like to find someone else who is what we are. And we always think that we will never be able to be like that being, because we get caught in the perspective of "him" and "me" instead of realizing that we are all that being. The process of visualizing an ideal master is one of the strongest transforming therapies that there is. In fact, the real masters are simply the living prototype of their ideal. This can only happen if the master is very close to that ideal, and that is, of course, very rare. It is terribly unfortunate that there are gurus who pose as something they are not, because there is nothing more disastrous to the soul of a person than realizing that his idol has feet of clay. He will never have trust in anyone else after that; it would be better if the guru had never started by giving him an idea of something to look up to. But what I am suggesting is that we have in ourselves the ability to project in front of ourselves the image of an ideal being. We can discover ourselves in our own projection of our real self in front of us. It is a process of self-discovery. But it is most important to have a very clear picture of the ideal being, because otherwise there is a tendency to slip back into one's personal consciousness or personal sense of identity.

It is very exciting to discover that simply by imagining an aura around one's body, one immediately increases the bioluminescence of the cells of the body: there is an action of the imagination even on the physical body. Previously, it was believed that such effects were just hallucinations and that people were just representing something that was not true, but now we know that simply by representing an image, we can bring about a change even in the cells of the body. The bioluminescence, which is caused by the photons released by the cells of the body, is immediately enhanced by an act of imagination.

In fact, many of our everyday activities are triggered off, or monitored by, visualizations. For example, all the motions needed to drive a car would be impossible to make if we thought about them; it is the visualization of where we want to go that monitors the brain patterning and the release of signals in the nervous system to bring about the muscular movements that make it possible to drive. This is also the principle of biofeedback; it is possible to heat the hands by imagining that one is holding a hot cup of tea. In the same way, blood pressure can be lowered, the heartbeat slowed, and some control exerted on the functions of the pancreas, the pituitary gland, and other organs and glands. This is the secret of psychosomatic medicine. But it cannot be done with the will. If we tried to act upon the secretions of the pancreas, to make it secrete more glycogen or insulin, we could not do it; when we try to slow down the heartbeat by our will, we cannot. But by representing to oneself, for example, the beat of the pendulum of a clock at a certain frequency and then visualizing the pulsing of the blood following the frequency of that clock, one can slow the heartbeat to synchronize it with that visualization. There are even doctors treating cancer by helping their patients to visualize changes in the DNA of cancerous growths.

There is a close relationship between the brain patterning and the secretions of the glands, and even of the enzymes within the cells; the brain patterning can even have an impact upon the DNA that can change the functioning of the whole body. The same principle applies in meditation: representing to ourselves a perfect being will immediately change our whole internal disposition and even affect the body. We can begin to identify ourselves with that being. One might say that that is a terrible ego trip, but the beauty of it is to be able to combine what Hazrat Inayat Khan calls the aristocracy of the spirit and the democracy of the ego. Once again, we combine opposites, just as we do when we realize that we are both the totality and part of the totality: we are perfect and yet imperfect, and so we must make a combination—the reconciliation of the irreconciliables.

THE IDEAL MASTER MEDITATION

Now you will have to make a fictitious pilgrimage with me to the Himalayas—not the earthly Himalayas, but the celestial Himalayas. You have left the world behind you and are full of anticipation; you have left even your being behind, and are climbing the footpaths in the mountains, meeting the pilgrims from all over India and the rest of the world. There are thousands of sannyasins, and a religious fervor is in the atmosphtere, particularly around the temples, some of which are very beautiful.

But now you wish to get away from the crowd of pilgrims, and you go off on your own, moving through the snow, perhaps moved by an eerie hunch; and then, suddenly, you notice that the whole of nature seems enchanted by some kind of magic, a kind of transfigured space. You feel a very strong atmosphere, or magnetism, coming from one spot, and as you look in that direction you see a sannyasin, a rishi, sitting in the middle of nature. But this is a purely fictitious being: not a representation of any master, saint, or prophet you may have heard or read about, or any master you may have met or known about; this is purely your own representation of your ideal guru. Imagine that there were many, many wonderful people from whom you could choose one who was the ideal guru, and represent to yourself what that ideal guru would be like. I advise, incidentally, that women would choose, if possible, a woman rishi—but this is only my advice. Men might also imagine a woman guru, because there are many wonderful gurus who are women in the world today. When I speak of a guru as "he" or "him," it is only for simplicity's sake.

You should now have a very clear picture of how you think your guru looks, even physically, in detail; his clothing, his bearing, and the glance of his eyes should be very clear. The first thing you notice is that the whole environment seems to be charged with his magnetism, which is tremendous; you yourself, sitting in his presence, feel magnetic and radiant with magnetic power—a power you could use for healing. Then you notice the atmosphere of his being as distinct from his magnetism, and although it is impossible to describe, you can feel yourself bathing in the atmosphere of his being, attuning yourself to it so that wherever you go you will be carrying that atmosphere with you. Now you notice that he seems to manifest a divine power: his whole being seems to be inhabited by a power that is a sort of majesty; his being is kingly. This great power is reminiscent of the words of Hazrat Inayat Khan when he says that you discover in yourself the power that moves the universe. It is the same power that moves the planets, the atom, the sea, the storm, and the sap in the trees—the power that can transform things. It gives you a kingly bearing, and when you look further into his countenance, he seems to be peering at you with an intense gaze.

The first thing you notice about his gaze is an intense light in his glance; in fact, his whole body seems to be surrounded by a brilliant aura, and everthing seems to be transfigured by that light. You yourself begin to feel transfigured, and you are aware of being a being of light. His light seems to illuminate your light, to make your light burn more strongly: you are sharing a communion of light with him. In his glance, you see that he seems to be looking right into your soul, with enormous wisdom and crystal-clear perspicacity. In the light of his intelligence you begin to see everything more clearly.

Now you notice that behind that very clear realization is the state of awakening. He is totally awake, totally aware; and so far, you have been sleeping, caught up in your confused understanding. Here you are in the presence of such a positive awareness that he seems to shake you by his very awakeness; he shakes you into awakening yourself, and now you begin to perceive his emotion. It is, of course, ecstasy: he seems to be lost in divine ecstasy, but when you look more deeply into it, you see that he has, in fact, a broken heart. He seems to share in the heart of the universe and to have a sensitivity to suffering that expresses itself in the form of compassion—a tremendous gentleness and compassion together with the power we saw before. And yet he is bubbling over with joy. There is a great seriousness in his glance, and, at the same time, there is humor and joviality —a victorious, glorious outburst of the sunshine of his soul, which is a very high quality of joy.

When you look deeper into his eyes, you see that behind all that you have seen there is a quality of peace, of serenity, and you see that he is totally free, not only from the world, but from himself—and that is what gives him his peace. And you feel that your own heart has been shattered into experiencing cosmic suffering, that your own being is bursting with jubilation at the sight of so much joy, that you feel freed from yourself through the impact of his freedom, and that you share in that peace beyond understanding.

Then you notice a kind of innocence in him—what we call the immaculate condition. And you yourself, in the presence of this person, feel your own being going through a cathar-sis; you feel your being becoming purified by the purity of his being and by the power of his truth. You become more and more genuine, more and more authentic; you are aware of the tremendous importance of becoming the truth. Then you realize that his being has become totally sacred; you discover in his manner the sacredness of embodying the divine perfection. And you, too, feel as though you have been granted something very holy, which you must protect against sacrilege—not only from outside, but from your own imperfection—and so you are transported, transfigured, and overwhelmed by the impact of this being upon you—so much so that you no longer have to sit in his presence anymore; you could sit anywhere in the forest and just let his being come through you. All those things that you expe-rienced are still there in you. In fact, they *are* you: you are sitting in the mountain vastness, and you are radiating life and magnetism, you are inhabited by a divine power and majesty, you are radiant with light, and you are pure lumi-nous intelligence, casting that light upon all things. You have become sensitive to the suffering of humanity and of all living creatures, and at the same time you are full of joy. Beyond that, you are free: no one can influence you, no one can hold you, no one can upset you, no one can insult you—you are free, and therefore manifest peace beyond under-standing. You are lost in divine ecstasy and are manifesting the heavenly spheres after having become purified in the immaculate state; you realize the tremendous gift of the divine grace, in the form of your soul, which you have to protect against all profanation. Do you realize that this is your real being? In fact, you could never have imagined the ideal master if you were not that: that being is known to you because it is your real self.

Chapter 9:

CREATIVITY: TAPPING IN TO THE THINKING OF THE UNIVERSE

When we are counseling ourselves, and others, we should know where the person we are counseling is in his forward march through life. The Sufis recognize seven, perhaps more, stages, or stations, on the path.

Roughly speaking, in the first stage one is like a butterfly; one enjoys playing with the flowers. As Hazrat Inayat Khan said, a child is sometimes so excited by the sight of fire that he would like to put hot coals in his pocket.

The second stage is one of increasing maturity. One feels one must accomplish something, pull his life together, have a family and a car and so forth—do all the done things, affirm the personality, have some kind of dominance over situations, and achieve some kind of accomplishment and fulfillment.

In the third stage, one begins to wonder why on earth one should exist if only to be a dollar-making machine. At this point, there is a growing need to know and to understand.

In the fourth stage, there is a tendency to become some-what burnt out. One becomes tired of all the sham, the selfishness and violence, and the dishonesty of people—the masquerade. One may also become very sensitive about people's emotions and about one's environment and the kind of music one likes to hear: there is a need for something very pure and very real, a need for authenticity. That is when one feels like climbing the high mountains and living among the rocks and snow; one cannot even stand the lush flowers in the valley. The need for utter simplicity may make one tend to shy away from people and from life and to be rather sensitive—to become like a deer that keeps escaping the city and going to the deep woods. It is only a stage; ideally, one comes right back into life again.

Hazrat Inayat Khan describes the later stages as being those in which one can just play with the children of the world, and if they tear out one's hair or kick or spit at one, it has no effect, because one has gone beyond all those things; if they kick and bite, maybe they just have to kick and bite. One bears no grudge against them. At that stage, we can say one has really made it.

People have different needs according to the different stages of their lives, and it is not difficult to understand that people who are in a rather flippant stage, who enjoy life just as it is and have not yet tasted of the suffering of humanity, are not aware of suffering and so can go on enjoying their dance until they come to grief—which, in fact, usually happens. But once a person has reached a certain stage of maturity, it is possible to get overwrought, overburdened, and overtaxed, and to have no idea of how to find peace anymore. We sometimes find that when people try to go on retreat they find it impossible to sit down quietly and meditate. They want to move—it goes counter to the grain for them to try to force themselves to sit quietly and to still the body and the mind. This is why I do not favor relaxation unless relaxation is compensated by awakening—by a very intense emotion or realization. There are some meditations that can be done in action. This is sometimes preferable, because it is not always wise to try to force people to go against the grain—and, in any case, some people simply cannot do it. If such a person is able to force his body to remain still, his mind may become more active and more restless than ever; and if he tries to force the mind to be still, then the mind is only gagged, and the emotions get into a turmoil. So we sometimes find that it takes three or four days or more for a person to adapt to the retreat state and to tone down his whole endocrine system. One method we use is to suggest that the retreatant walk in the forest and try to experience the life of the beings around him instead of closing himself up in his personal ivory tower. Gradually, he brings himself into harmony with all things, and then he can find peace in himself.

In an extreme situation—one that borders on the pathological or is pathological—we often find that a person has been badly pummeled by grief and pain and disappointment. Or perhaps he is in a situation where he can turn neither left nor right: whichever way he turns, he is jammed. In a case like that, the whole psychophysiological mechanism gets totally out of gear. We might make an analogy by imagining that the human being is a very gently poised mechanism, with a built-in device—the autonomic control —that we could compare with a thermostat. A thermostat is a feedback system: it picks up information from the environment, namely fluctuations in temperature, and uses this information to keep the temperature constant by increasing or decreasing the amount of combustion in a furnace. If the whole system has been overtaxed and the thermostat is blown, it can no longer control the system. And there is no way of controlling that system by one's will. This is something we must be aware of, because we are following the path of mastery and so need to know how we can find some way in which the will can insert itself into the mechanism at some stage and set it right.

This phenomenon may manifest as compulsion, particularly obsessive thoughts; a person may not be able to stop thinking about the thing that grieves him. He may want to stop thinking about it, but cannot because it is just too strong; however hard he may try to muster his will against it, the will proves inadequate to the task. And there is no use trying to calm a person down; forcing him by using sedatives is going against the grain, and the body tends to react against it. The use of sedatives tends to do violence to the being of the person, even though in many cases it is the only feasible method, because otherwise a person can get so out of control that he is a danger to himself and to society. And all our methods of meditation break down totally; there is no way to exercise control. So we must find another way to deal with such a person.

In India, elephants occasionally go mad. The cause of their madness is not psychic; elephants go mad when they have been insulted or hurt in their sense of self-esteem, or when they have been trapped in such a way that they know there is no way out. The "thermostat" explodes, and there is no more control. An elephant in this state will attack his keeper and everything and everyone else in sight. The only person who can approach a mad elephant is a *madjhub*—a dervish —a person who is equally as mad as the elephant. The elephant seems, in fact, to enjoy the company of such a person who is considered a madman by other people but who has a sanity that most people do not understand. I have said that the dervish can see through the hearts of all beings, and the reason he can calm the elephant is that he does not try to calm the elephant: he gives him ecstasy, and that is the only cure for the elephant's madness.

There is an enormous amount of energy being generated in many types of pathology, and we cannot simply smother this energy. If it is channeled into a peak experience, that may be the only solution. That is why, in India, some people are able to find a *modus vivendi* only at the side of the holy man—one who had dedicated himself totally to the spiritual life.

If we are in our ordinary consciousness and facing a person who has passed the threshold into another world that is unknown to the ordinary person, we are trying to influence or control him, and from his point of view doing violence to him, because he has to find his way through that maze. He is overwhelmed by the unleashing of psychic forces and images, which are emerging in his mind with tremendous power. He may be hearing voices, which is to say, interpreting to his mind the strength of the imposters that are working through him; we may find him shouting back at his "voices" and not know what he is shouting at, while for him the experience is real. We cannot reach him, and he does not want to be reached. This is an extreme example, which we know must follow its course; and, curiously enough, the physio-psychological organism of the body has a capacity for self-repair, as long as it is not interfered with in a way that makes matters worse. And some of the things that we do to mental patients are indeed just that—making matters worse.

There is a normal, inbuilt mechanism whereby the pituitary secretes endorphins, which are a kind of organic morphine. If this mechanism is allowed to work unimpeded, the human being can provide enough tranquilizers out of his own organism to defeat the attack upon himself. But as we have remarked, this organism does not work perfectly, because it is very gently poised; it can easily be disrupted. However there is a way whereby we can repattern the brain so that the whole endocrine system will follow suit and the whole disruptive mechanism can be adjusted. One method, which we have discussed, is visualization, which manipulates the whole functioning of the nervous system and which touches upon the most crucial mechanism in the whole being, which is creativity. This is why it is often helpful to encourage a person who has alienated himself from the environment to project himself in painting, drawing, or music, or doing something creative with his hands. This form of therapy has proven to be most useful because it is encouraging creativity.

We can discriminate between two factors in our way of thinking. One is reacting to the environment, or processing the environment. In this mode, we are actually transforming experience into information; it is like a process of digestion. Whatever has happened has been assimilated, and although one sometimes does not remember very much of what has happened, the gist of it has been incorporated in one's being. This is data processing and storing, and it comprises much of our thinking, which is simply our way of reacting to the environment and processing the thoughts of other people.

The other mode of thought is purely creative thought that has not been promoted, or even catalyzed, by anything from outside. Creative thought may be catalyzed, but most creative of all thoughts are the ones that descend upon us out of the clear blue sky. We do not know what the system of the process of association that led to it is; it may have been catalyzed by a situation or a thought, but it is not a reaction. In fact, it is the capability of the human being to tap into the thinking of the universe which is the greatest miracle.

In experiments with rats, it has been found that sometimes, when they have a choice between a sure way of finding food and exploring, they choose to explore. The exploratory drive in human beings is extremely important, because it is, exactly, creativity. It is trying out new ways of doing things and new combinations.

Arthur Koestler said that the pull of the future is stonger

than the weight of the past. That explains why the purpose is more important than the cause, and why, in counseling patients, it is useful up to a point to examine causes, but it is much more useful to see where events are leading or how the human being is finding his own way of self-repair and, perhaps, floundering in his attempts to do so and losing himself. The urge to explore can lead a person astray if he meanders in the realms of fantasy rather than imagination: fantasy is not imagination.

In a state of reverie, we sometimes find that there are some thoughts that seem random and other thoughts that are meaningful. If a person is not used to dealing with this state and does not know how to distinguish between the two, he can easily let himself be led into the random areas of thought instead of the truly creative ones. As we have said, the question of randomness in the universe is a metaphysical problem. In physics, it looks as though there is randomness where there is entropy—where matter is disintegrating and decaying. But there is also the principle of "order out of disorder"—while we may not know the behavior of the different molecules of gas under certain circumstances, the total pressure remains constant. Somehow, although we may not know how He does it, God is able to make order out of disorder.

In Zoroastrianism, there is a belief that however strong evil is, good will always predominates in the end, because order is safeguarded against disorder; this is affirmed in the popular saying, "If you give the devil a long enough rope, he'll hang himself." So we do not know whether what we call randomness is simply our inability to see the meaningfulness of events. However, what remains more interesting is the ability to earmark those thoughts that are meaningful in the whole array of thoughts. How can we distinguish between fantasy and imagination? This is a very important criterion: for example, an artist may throw a little bit of paint anywhere on his canvas and his work may sell for a million dollars, while another artist may be expressing a rather complex order. The difference between the two is not always clear; our ability to assess the value of a piece of art is not always that good. There are some pieces of music that are a little bit random: the composer is indulging in fantasy, and if we changed a note no one would know the difference. But if anyone were to change a note in a toccata and fugue of Bach, everyone would notice the difference.

In a previous discussion of the divine programming of the universe, we saw that we are that programming. That program is not set. It is always inventive, creative, exploratory, and moving forward. But this seems to be most true of the main thrust of creativity, which seems to branch off into blind alleys, just as the main stream of a river can sometimes branch off into dead ends. Many people who would like to believe that everything is God find it difficult to see God in a particular person; they feel as if the divine programming had gone wrong in that instance. So we might say that there are degrees of "Godness" just as there are degrees of centrality in our bodies: if we cut off our hair or our fingernails, it does not affect our being very much, whereas the loss of brain cells can have a very traumatic effect. The main reality seems to be watered down at its jagged ends; and, in the same way, the main thrust of creativity can be dispersed in fantasy. Fantasy could be anything: there is no real meaningfulness in fantasy, and meaningfulness is the true criterion of creativity. It is meaningfulness that makes us choose between fantasy and imagination. The question of meaningfulness is very important for intuition, and when we are creating, it is our sense of authenticity that is at work.

People who have a great scruple about truthfulness do not indulge in fantasy. That means that although they may not be controlling their thoughts with their will, they are in some way watching over the flow of their thoughts to keep them within the mainstream and not allow them to deviate from it.

When the whole psycho-physiological system is overcome, then a person can be so overwhelmed with thoughts that there is no way of making any distinction between those that are meaningful and those that are not. There is no way of intervening with the personal will, because the "thermostat"—the autonomic system—is itself hooked to another "thermostat," which in turn is hooked to still another; the interplay between the psycho-physiological systems resembles several computers hooked together, not simply one that could be controlled by the personal will. But there is a way of allowing a greater will to take over the entire system, and that is the great art of knowing how to bring about change in a person—as long as the process of destruction has not gone too far.

We should note that there is, in fact, a double system of "thermostats," and we should distinguish between them. The subconscious and the superconscious have been put in one bag under the term "unconscious," but we should distinguish between the two. The difference is between the cosmic and the transcendent dimensions of consciousness. For example, animals are endowed with a built-in alarm system. While we still do not know how they transmit signals, we do know that animals, and even fish and insects, are able to transmit signals to one another in a kind of "yes-or-no" system that communicates danger or safety—a simple system based, apparently, on whether one feels good or bad about a situation. That is a subconscious mechanism. A superconscious mechanism would be one that is not just a "yes-or-no" system but a kind of supercontrol over the whole mechanism of one's body and mind. This is something that one can reach in a higher state of consciousness.

When another person is overwrought by suffering or pain or obsessive thoughts, he is unable to reach his higher consciousness; the only way we can help him to do so is by being in a very high state of consciousness ourselves. A person who has alienated himself from the world of actuality has a very sure intuition, and if he feels that we are still in the "trip" he has escaped from, he will not believe we can help him. He doesn't want to go back to that place, and he can see quite clearly if we are there: he need only look into our eyes to know that we cannot help him. But if we have really attained our higher consciousness, then he recognizes something that is known to him and is meaningful to him, and there is a possibility that we will be able to maintain the lines of communication by being in that state of consciousness in the actual world. In this way, we can build a bridge between the two for him.

It would be a great mistake, however, to pit our own peacefulness against the patient's agitation, because there is a tendency for a desperate person to reject help. The defense mechanisms of the mind and body are not adjusted to receive the help that would be good for that person; cancer patients, for example, very often begin to lose weight despite the fact that their cells are proliferating, because the glandular system is inhibiting food intake: they cannot take in the one thing they need most. In the same way, although a disturbed person needs peace, he will reject peace if we try to give it to him. It is better to begin by attuning ourselves to his consciousness and then gradually slowing down the rhythm until he is able to attune himself to our state, if he will respond. The same principle applies in working with children: if a child is "wired," it is impossible to calm him just by imposing one's own peace; one should first attune oneself to the child and then slow down the rhythm. In the case of a disturbed person, of course, this may still involve overcoming a great deal of initial resistance on the patient's part.

This is why I believe that ecstasy works better than peace. The dervish is able to help the mad elephant better than a peaceful man, because the dervish is not a man of peace.

He's full of fire—laughing and crying at the same time. Our methods of relaxation are not adequate to the task, even though the relaxed state is the desired end—although not even the entire desired end, because relaxation must be compensated by a very high state of awakening.

There is a difference between ecstasy and euphoria. Euphoria is emotion that can become disruptive and cause a person to burn out; it is a form of ecstasy that has gone out of control and yet at the same time is tied to outer events —an emotion that can be indulged in only as long as things in the outer world go well. The emotion of ecstasy comes from being in tune with the ecstasy of the universe rather than enjoying our own little tempest in a teacup. I have suffered several terrible tragedies in the course of my life; in the worst case, I cured myself of my depression by playing Bach's Mass in B Minor every night. I feel sure that any effort on my part to reach peace would have failed; in fact, the Mass in B Minor is not peaceful, but it does reach peace at the end, in the "Dona Nobis Pacem." The mass goes through a long process before it brings us into peace: Bach clearly had a great knowledge of human emotions. The meaningfulness of it all is that it links us with cosmic emotions, and then our emotions seem insignificant. This is the only way to break the vicious circle. We cannot reason with a person who is caught in his own little vicious circle, so we must give him something that is meaningful. Then he can let go of whatever it is that is perturbing him so much. This is why the Cosmic Celebration is so important.

We have tended to rob our lives of their main attribute, which is glorification. It is for the purpose of glorification that there have been ceremonies in the churches—the marches and processions, the prayers and lights and music. These elements form a scenario that places a person in a certain frame of mind, and particularly in a frame of emotion, or an attunement of emotion, that is conducive to the fulfillment of his greatest need. Nowadays, many of those elements of the church service have been cut out, and we are more likely to hear a sermon about politics. The glorification is gone, and then one may begin to think that it was all superstition, like a belief in the angels. Of course, it is important to deal with the problems of the earth plane, but those problems have their counterpart in transcendent realms: it is all reality. We cannot segregate one aspect of a problem from its roots—or from its halo of glory. It is all part of a oneness.

But since the old forms of glorification no longer seem to work, we need to find ways to replace them. This is why we in the Sufi Order organize a Cosmic Celebration several times a year, with up to three hundred people on stage. Sometimes we are able to really succeed in creating a cosmic ecstasy, and the moment when we are most successful comes when, instead of producing a drama, we find ourselves really praying. It is at those moments that we find ourselves tapping in to resources beyond our ordinary scope —rather like the woman who lives in the suburbs of London who, without having had any musical education at all, writes wonderful compositions in the style of Chopin or Schubert or Beethoven. Hazrat Inayat Khan speaks about this storehouse of knowledge to which we have access. We can call this intuition, in fact, because we cannot have access to it if we are using our ordinary judgement. To reach that place, we must throw away our crutches altogether.

When I am giving *darshan*—using my intuition to look into the souls of my students—I find myself rather disoriented at first because in this process one must trust oneself totally to what is coming through to one, and in one's mind one wonders how one could dare say something one isn't sure about in one's mind. What one says in such a situation may change a person's life if he acts on it, and even if one is right ninety-nine times, the one time one is wrong one may do a great deal of harm to a person. So it takes a lot of gall to fall back on one's intuition. Eventually, from the feedback, one learns to trust one's intuition. When intuition does not involve other people, it is not so fraught: when one is wrong, one is oneself the loser. But when other people are involved, then one must have very great scruples, and one might like to be able to use some supporting evidence from the signs that strike one's mind.

We know that we can sometimes tell from a person's face if he is going through a trauma, or see in his eyes if he is sincere or not, or is facing himself or failing to face life. There are many outward indications: phrenology, handwriting, the way a person dresses. But these signs are not one hundred percent reliable, and even if we take them into consideration we will be able to make only limited deductions. If we rely on these signs, we cannot use our intuition. In the case of the young man who had set fire to a hospital, the signs were that he was innocent; it was my intuition that told me he was not. So we must really trust our intuition. The problem is that although we would like to trust our intuition, when we find out we were wrong we feel it would be silly to trust it any further unless we can improve our ability to use it.

One method we can use to improve our intuition is to check when our hunches were verified and when they were not, and then try to remember the state we were in when we had an intuition that was right. This method is like biofeedback: we do not know how to change our heartbeat, but we are able to change the position of the needle on a biofeedback machine that shows us we have changed our heartbeat. We don't know how we do it, but we do the things that are necessary to move the needle, which gives us information about what is happening in our body. Intuition works the same way: we do not know what we do to get ourselves into a state in which we are able to have intuition, but we remember which state we were in when our intuition was verified and then gradually learn to trust ourselves. Of

course, this is a different state from our ordinary consciousness. But is it possible to be in both states at the same time?
Can we be active, typing, for example, and at the same time
have one part of our being in a receptive state so that we can
pick up an intuition? The answer is yes. It is very difficult,
but it is possible.

In our ordinary way of communicating, we think of another person as being "over there" while we are "here," and
we judge a person, as psychologists know very well, by his
behavior and appearance. Our experience of him is through
his behavior rather than our experience of his experience.
We are reaching him in time and space. We are not really
communicating with him totally, but only through the me-
dium of his behavior, and consequently we are passing
judgement upon him.

When we are using intuition, we have to apply the principle of cosmic consciousness. There is a transfer of our center
from us to the other person, and then all that we know is
how he thinks or feels. This does not mean that we know
the answer to his problems; if he does not know it, we
cannot know it by getting into his consciousness. But if we
get into the transcendent dimension and therefore into his
higher consciousness—the unmanifest, or that which is not
yet manifested in him but which is on its way—then we can
see the divine planning behind it all. That is the answer: to
get into the divine planning. But in doing this, we should
also do quite the opposite at the same time, which is to feel
how we feel in ourselves and how we react to him. In other
words, although we have said that we transfer our center
from ourselves to him, we are looking within ourselves
rather than reaching him outside. We do not reach him in
time and space, we reach him from inside ourselves: we can
no longer think of him as "over there."

We are gifted with a very sensitive kind of barometer
inside ourselves, which Hazrat Inayat Khan calls the spirit.

We can elucidate the meaning of that word for ourselves by its use in the expressions "to kill someone's spirit" and "to be in a high spirit." When we have done something we are not happy about, our spirit is heavy, weighed down, encumbered. When we have done something heroic or have overcome something in ourselves—our hatred for someone, for example—our spirit is high. The secret of ecstasy is to make one's spirit high.

When we are very sensitized in our spirit, we react to the presence of a person in a very clear way. We will always feel in ourselves what that person is, because everything is in us; if that person is insincere, we are aware of those aspects of ourselves that are insincere when we say, "Oh, how nice to see you," and do not really mean it. If that person is violent, we will feel the violence in ourselves. This is the elementary school of intuition.

At a more advanced stage, we may find ourselves dealing with a person who intends to do something and wishes to know whether he should do it or not. As I have said, we are not supposed to advise people to do or not to do anything, except in an extreme case such as that of the young man whom I advised to become a photographer. In that case the man was going to commit suicide, so it was necessary that someone intervene. In any case, whether we say anything or not, the person questioning us can feel how we feel in ourselves about his project, because he is probing into our soul.

What is really involved here is the divine programming, and the question is whether the person's undertaking really flows with the main course of the divine programming and will, therefore, be successful. But it is a more complicated question than we think, because his will, or initiative, is also part of the divine programming, and we know that it is sometimes well worthwhile to take the trouble to steer one's boat upstream instead of downstream—although that will not be successful if there is not enough fuel to do it. It is simply easier to float downstream, and if a person wishes to challenge this, that does not mean he is wrong; the divine will is complex, and it includes our wills. But we can feel if that person is going to run out of fuel and hence come to grief, and if we know this, we have a responsibility to warn him. If we see a piece of debris in the middle of a busy road that is posing a hazard, we have the responsibility of telling the police or stopping and removing the debris or otherwise acting to remove the risk; it is terribly irresponsible simply to go on and assume that things will take care of themselves. We have a responsibility to warn a person who has asked us for advice.

People often come to me because they want to get married, and I find myself thinking, "Oh, no, they'll never make it." But if I told them not to get married, I would be putting negative thoughts in their minds. Sometimes when people ask me if I think they're really made for each other, I tell them that if they really love one another, they will not let themselves be influenced by my opinion; they'll go ahead and get married whether I advise them to or not. That is the best criterion. But people are very much in need of guidance in life, and where our intuition gives us a sense of urgency, my rule of not giving advice breaks down. My rule is valid only if we are using the mind. Then I would say we should be very careful about advising people. But if our intuition is absolutely genuine—which is very difficult to ascertain, but, as we have noted, can be determined by our sense of authenticity—then a warning is like the divine guidance that is telling us to warn a person against doing something that will not be successful. There is no such thing as prediction. We cannot predict how things are going to be, because the divine plan is not fixed—it is not preordained. There are laws of probability; under certain circumstances the chances are greater or lesser that a certain thing will happen. We can choose the situations that seem to offer greater chances of success. But even if a project meets with obstacles, that does not mean that it is not right; sometimes we must be quite persevering and keep on at it even to the point of being cussed about it. If we are convinced that it is right and feel right about it in ourselves, then it is like the toccatas and fugues of Bach—totally orderly: it makes sense. If we do not feel right about it, it is probably out of step; it does not make sense, or perhaps we might say it does not contribute towards the forward march of civilization.

It was during my last retreat in India, at the source of the Ganges, that I found myself looking into the divine programming and seeing that although it appears as if it could go in any direction because it is so inventive and creative, instead of just going anywhere or dispersing, it is marshalled: the DNA of the universe becomes man; it is hominized. The programming of the universe is definitely purpose-oriented. The same thing is true of our plans. If our plans make sense in terms of the forward march of humanity in improving its abilities, then we can feel that we are on the road to success. But if our plans are out of step or are overstressing our capacities, then we come to grief, like the young man who wanted to be an author. He did not have the capacity to be an author, but mastering photography helped him develop the power he then used to become an author. If a person overstresses himself and runs into a defeat, he loses his self-confidence. It is better to undertake something that is less challenging and then give it up and undertake something more challenging.

When we approach events intuitively, we find that processes go in cycles. There are certain moments when energy is reaching upwards, which are called *uruj* in Sufism. We can make an analogy with surfing: there is a certain moment when one can slip onto a wave as it is rising and so let the wave carry one. But if one hits the wave when it is receding, then one can only sink. In the same way, a person who has his own plan must ask how well this plan meshes with the way things are flowing; he must find the right groove to slip into to become part of the forward march. This is something that we feel.

When a person's energy is what the Sufis call *nazul*—when it is declining—then the constellation of the whole situation is not favorable, and however much he may fight, the forces of declination will be stronger than his ability to overcome them. This is also something that we feel. When a person begins to decline, that is a sign that he should jump off and try to catch the next wave. We find this state in people who hang on to their jobs when they are no longer functioning well in them and it is time for them to begin to do something else. At other times, we feel that it is better not to "switch horses in the middle of the stream"—when we are on the rising wave and, even if we think of doing something else, we should wait until we have reached the top of the wave to spring onto the next one. These are all things that we feel. There is no way of assessing them with the mind. When people come to a therapist and ask questions about how they are to proceed, the therapist finds that they often take the wrong decisions—that they play their cards badly when they have an advantage and do not know it. In a sense, the therapist is their safeguard, and the only way he or she can help them is by really having a sense of the direction in which things are flowing—the purpose. It is a question of being in harmony—which is not the same thing as toeing the line.

The composer Gounod was able to write a theme that could be superimposed on the first prelude of Bach's *Well-Tempered Klavier,* although one might have thought that prelude was totally complete in itself. We might consider that prelude to be the way things are flowing in life, and that a person who wonders what his place is in all this can somehow find a theme that flows with it all and is able to integrate itself totally. Then he can be successful.

Chapter 10:

REGRESSION AND ANTICIPATION, CAUSE AND PURPOSE

Very often a practitioner of psychotherapy has cause to wonder to what extent one is really permitted to intervene and to what extent one should let a patient learn by himself. Obviously, whenever two people are communicating, whether in an ordinary conversation or in a consulting room, there cannot but be an interaction between them, and, therefore, some impact of the therapist upon the patient—as well as some impact of the patient upon the therapist.

My father died when I was ten, and he was so busy that I seldom had any opportunity to talk to him, but on one occasion I just broke through and asked him, "Abba, since one's opinion about some things can never be absolutely valid, should one never do anything, since by doing things one is intervening on the strength of a judgement?" I was about ten years old then, and, I am sure, put the question in less sophisticated terms than this, but that is about what I asked. He said, "By not intervening, you are just as responsible as if you were intervening, so there is no way of getting out of it. If the house is on fire or there is a log across the road—wherever there is a danger—if you do not warn people, you are responsible. There is no way of getting out of it: you have to intervene."

I began by saying "Do not intervene." In the last chapter, I said one must not intervene with one's rational mind, but that one can go by one's intuition. I have also said that the person himself cannot assume control over his mechanism, but that there is a way of bringing control through on the bias, as it were. The same applies to the therapist: he cannot control or in any way regulate the thinking of a patient by his thought, by his will, or by trying to show a straight way. But we cannot discount the impact of one being upon another; and the best thing the therapist can do is to sow seeds that that person will sustain and nourish in his being and that will eventually bear fruit. And this can be done in an unobtrusive way.

The crux of the matter is the relationship between events and one's qualities. One method that often proves to give excellent results is to put a person through a regression. We must be careful about it; it is a method that has been rather abused in rebirthing, but it is still valid. This means putting the person through a process of memory, so that he remembers what he did yesterday, the day before yesterday, a week ago, a month ago, a year ago, ten years ago—right back into his childhood, and possibly even his babyhood and even prior to that. When one tries to recall not only events but also how one felt in the midst of those events, one is moving away from the here and now—the world of actuality—and the consequence of that is that there is a change in the focus of consciousness. Consciousness is much less centered in the ego center; it gets scattered—decentered—and, therefore, one enters into a state resembling reverie. As a matter of fact, this is one method used in hypnosis to get a person into a subliminal state of consciousness. I am not in favor of hypnosis, but autohypnosis is somewhat better: one can, at least, compensate the sinking of consciousness by an awakening of consciousness.

What is absolutely essential to the method of regression is to make a person recall not only the events, but the qualities and the kinds of personalities that he assumed in the past. What was he like ten years ago? What was he like when he was a child? It is not only the events outside, but one's own qualities that determine the final impact. We can reverse the regression and see how the person has evolved in the course of time and establish the lines of communication between the two. For example, we might feel, "If I had been then the way I am now, things would not have happened the way they did; but if I am now the way I am, it is largely due to that event, which brought about a change in my being." There is an interaction of the way one was with the situation; those are parallel occurrences that move in a parallel way. Once one has established the connection between them, the whole thing can be applied to the present, and we can ask, "What are the qualities that I am being tested in by the divine planning, that I must develop in order to meet this situation?" That is the key. Instead of saying, "It's terrible, fate has been so unkind to me," and so on, we should ask, "What are the qualities I'm supposed to develop now?" Once we can get a person to ask this question of himself, he can proceed into what I call self-repair— and, what is more, self-regeneration or self-creation.

Self-creation involves a question that is at the heart of the process of regression. Regression can be followed up until we experience ourselves as we were in our parents—which, curiously enough, is perfectly true, because our bodies are not just bodies that have inherited the traits of our parents, they *are* the bodies of our parents, which continue to live in our bodies. And this includes not only our parents, but our grandparents and ancestors right back into the animal kingdom and the plant kingdom. The number of ancestors one has gets larger and larger as one moves back, and eventually it is infinite. The number of ancestors each of us theoretically had in the time of Moses is staggering—in fact, it is far greater than the number of human beings that were on the planet at that time. So we really do inherit from the whole universe. Aldous Huxley said, "Man is the spearhead of the forward march of the planet," but perhaps we should say, "of the universe." The whole past continues to live in us. Of course, only some of the characteristics of our ancestors are dominant. Most of them are recessive. That means they have not been activated; they are latent. They are just like the DNA in the cells of any part of the body: most of the genes are repressed by what are called "repressor enzymes," so that only some of them are active, and in this way their function is specialized in the formation of particular organs. The rest are inactive. In the same way, we inherit the richness of the whole universe. *We are it.* Not only do we inherit it; we *are* the richness that has to crowd into the capacity we offer it. The only way it can crowd into that capacity is by most of it remaining latent, while only some of it is active; but the latent qualities can be activated at any time. This can happen even with the cells of the body: at any time, if the repressor is taken away, the cells begin to develop in ways that are predictable. But this inheritance is only one of the factors of our formation; we must also take into account other forms of inheritance, which we might call the angelic dimension of our inheritance.

I know I am on thin ice here; people would like to know how one can prove that there is such a thing, or how one could know if there were. Yet in the same way that we can remember something that happened to our parents that they never told us, or something that happened to our ancestors, we can remember the great festivities in the heavens, because we carry that memory in us. So I sometimes like to ask,

"*Do* you remember the processions in the heavens?" We have all had the experience of feeling that we have already known a place or a person; we may feel when we meet someone that we have already met this extraordinary person, or we may find ourselves in Jerusalem and think, "That's strange, I know that I know this very chapel. I know even the wallpaper in this chapel." In the same way, we can have a feeling of déjà vu when we come across something that is very meaningful to us and that reminds us of the heavens. For example, in watching a sunrise we can feel, "This is home. I remember all this light! It's very extraordinary that I should have forgotten all about it here, but I remember—that was the way things used to be. Everything was lighted, and I have been plunged in this darkness all this time. Now here it is—that is my real home." Or we might look into the eyes of a baby and think, "This reminds me of those realms from which I have come." I often feel what a pity it is that the beautiful, candid innocence and light in the eyes of a child get lost. People seem to retrogress instead of advancing in life. If only we could keep our original innocence! We lose it because we have to fight in life and become sullied by all the dirt and filth in life, and eventually we get disenchanted and become cynical and lose the beautiful, natural disposition of the child. This is why it is so wonderful if we talk to a person who has become alienated from his heavenly origin and are somehow able to strike a note of memory—and all of a sudden he smiles, and in that smile his whole heavenly past comes through, just for a moment. This is the greatest therapy there is: to reconcile a person with his most important truths.

The Sufi center on the Lower East Side of New York is like an oasis in the middle of hell. There is screaming on the streets and the wail of sirens; many of the people one sees there are drugged or drunk. One can scarcely walk in the street without being accosted and harassed. At first, there is a tendency to be judgemental and to think of the terrible decadence and violence of humanity. But if one can get into the hearts of those people and really communicate with them, one realizes that these are people who are scuttling themselves because they have been hurt in their deepest core. They have been made to believe in something, and now they see that it is not true—like a child who has been told about Santa Claus and then suddenly discovers that there is no such thing as Santa Claus, and feels that he has been fooled. These are people who have started off with an ideal, and life has been so hard that they have lost that ideal and believe that they have been fooled. They don't want to hear all those highfalutin' words about spirituality, because for them it is just mystification.

The only way to help people like this is to be what one says, rather than say about what one is not, because they can spot insincerity and sanctimoniousness more quickly than anyone else. Preaching is the very thing they rebel against, because they have a great sense of authenticity. That is why the mad elephant will only tolerate the *madjhub*—because the dervish is real. He is not masquerading or putting on a show: he is what he is.

We all have it in us to rediscover our heavenly inheritance. This is, in fact, the teaching of Christ and of all the religions. But, as Hazrat Inayat Khan said, people are the followers of the followers, not the followers of the prophets. We might even say that people are the followers of the followers of the followers, because the teachings get so watered down.

In order to discover ourselves, we have to find ourselves in another ourself: it is events that trigger off the memory of the heavens. We cannot sit down and try to remember our heavenly inheritance, because it will not work that way. But if one is sensitive to music, for example, and listens to the sacred music of Thomas Tallis or William Byrd, or even

Monteverdi or Victoria, and if one can see what Bach is saying in his High Mass, then it will remind one of something familiar, and all of a sudden it will all come up again by the process of association, just as the sight of a flower can remind us of a person who once gave us that flower. The whole memory is unleashed.

I was once lecturing on this very subject in Paris on a Sunday afternoon, and just as I was speaking about the processions in the heavens, a small party of young boys marched past playing trumpets and drums. The synchronicity of their act and my words was perfect; in that moment, they brought home to the people listening exactly what I was describing. Sometimes the synchronicity of events brings us in touch with just the herb or medicine we need for our cure, as it were. We could find it in watching a beautiful sunset or seeing the smile of a child. Or we might be walking the streets in despair and suddenly hear music from a cathedral and think, "Ah, this is it." We find that music so much more meaningful than anything else that we feel we just have to walk into that cathedral. That is what saves us from despair. And the reason it is meaningful to us is because it is already known to us. We are only rediscovering something that is known to us. But we have to come across it outside ourselves in order to rediscover it inside ourselves. In the East, this is monitored by the presence of a rishi or holy man who does not have to remember the heavenly condition because he is aware of the heavenly condition here and now, which is much better. But perhaps the first step is to remember, and then re-establish the lines of communication with the heavenly realms.

There is often something artificial about therapy. It can be somewhat like a scientific experiment in which the therapist is segregating a phenomenon from its context so that it is not functioning the way it would normally. Therapy often creates artificial conditions—such as, for instance, having a patient lie down. Lying down promotes the unconscious, but not the superconscious; one finds oneself probing into a state of reverie—those unconscious worlds where some images are meaningful and some are not—and the psychiatrist is trying to let this happen without intervening. Viktor Frankl uses a method that I find preferable, in which he makes the patient sit up instead of lie down, and anticipate the future rather than turn back into the past. Instead of the cause, he investigates the purpose.

One of Frankl's patients was a woman who was about to commit suicide. She had a son who was infirm, and her second son had died; she no longer saw any purpose in her life. Frankl told her, "Imagine that it is twenty years hence, and you are looking back upon your life, and you remember how you were at this instant. Or go even further back and look at what you have done for your infirm child to help him come out of himself and adapt himself to life. In that state, will you think that your life was useless?" And at that moment, she saw the meaningfulness of her life. This is exactly what we call in Sufism "living one's resurrection in anticipation." It gives us a sense of purpose, which is the most important thing in our lives.

So regression has its place, although it is moving back in time. But we can also reverse regression and earmark qualities in ourselves that have been inherited from a particular parent, which is a process of self-awareness. Rediscovering the heavenly planes can be part of a regression, but it could lead towards the experience of the heavenly counterpart of our being now, instead of then. This is a movement into the present—or the eternal—and it should be completed by the opposite of regression, which is projecting ourselves forward and looking back upon the present. The Sufis say, "Die before death and resurrect now." Resurrection is not in the dimension of becoming; it is in the dimension of time that goes from the process of becoming into eternity. It is the eternalizing of that which is transient, and it is moving into the eternal—the everywhere and always—instead of the here and now—like an inverted cone or pyramid.

Occasionally people who are experiencing regression and trying to bring their memory past the threshold of their birth and into the womb of their mother find themselves regressing into their previous incarnations instead of into their ancestors. This poses the question of whether there really is such a thing as reincarnation and whether such experiences prove that there is. There are many different theories about reincarnation, and we can at least acknowledge that it is not only our ancestors who continue to live in us, but also something new that is formed out of a process of cross-pollenization. We also are not simply our previous incarnations, although there is a continuity there as well.

My theory of reincarnation is that when a person dies and no longer has the use of his body, he goes on functioning in other realms; perhaps he is a djinn or an angel. In this state, he may meet another djinn or angel and procreate—create a new infant djinn or angel. That infant may then incarnate on the earth plane in a being who carries some of the inheritance of the person who has died and "reincarnated." The person who has died continues to live on another plane, even though part of him has reincarnated. He or she may, in fact, have several "children" on that plane, so there may be several human beings who are the reincarnation of one person. But we must not think that we are definitely a particular historical person. There are many influences that criss-cross, interfuse, and intermesh to form one's being. Teilhard de Chardin said that we are the point upon which multiple threads of the universe converge—the point of convergence of a whole network; and the poet Saint-Exupéry said that life is a network of relationships.

As we know, a geometric point has no volume and, therefore, no frontier. The same is true of us: we are a point of convergence inasmuch as we look upon ourselves as an ego, but in fact that point of convergence incorporates the totality of the network. There is no frontier of our being. The realization of this gives us the greatest optimism. There is no limit to our being; the limit is only in the mind. There is no limit in fact. Discovering all the dimensions of our being is the greatest source of optimism and is the surest way of breaking down all the blocks. That is the great secret; we could say it is the liberation from the limited notion of the self. The sky is the limit.

Chapter 11:

TRANSFORMATION

Regression is useful only if it is accompanied by awareness of the transformation in one's being in relationship to
events and only if it gets to its real point, which is the
question, "What are the qualities that I'm supposed to develop, and how do I develop those qualities?" The only way
to develop them is to discover that they are already in us and
to be able to earmark them in ourselves. For instance, a
person may think that he does not have any self-confidence,
but that is not true; it's just the way he thinks. He has just
as much power in him as anyone else. He may not know it
is there, or know how to find it; but it is there all the same.

The objective of psychoanalysis is very often to make a
person see where he is blocked. This can be helpful, but
sometimes all one needs is a little more power in his system
to overcome a block; if he cannot remove the block, he can
at least find more power in himself and then simply overcome it. Psychosynthesis is much more important than analysis, because in it the therapist can give the patient
something instead of telling him why things have gone
wrong.

When Christ spoke about our divine inheritance, he said, "Be ye perfect as your Father in heaven is perfect." Hazrat Inayat Khan once said that if you are conscious of your inheritance you can claim it. Goethe said, "That which you have inherited from your ancestors, you must conquer yourself in order to possess." Those qualities are there, but we still have to conquer them. That is, I think, the main objective of psychotherapy: to make a person aware of what he is as well as making him aware of the blocks he has. And what he is includes all that we have discussed, plus the divine inheritance, which is the most important element of all. That is something that we experience in samadhi. In my last retreat, I made a point of not going too high into samadhi, because then one arrives at a state like deep sleep, where there is no more awareness of any thoughts: it is simply pure intelligence, beyond causality. It is better to slow down when we get higher up, so that we can experience what we have always been since the beginning of time. This experience is relative, of course, because there are relative levels of eternity. In the higher state of samadhi, one has gone beyond time and space, but at the causal level there is a different cycle of time—what we might call the cycle of becoming. In this state, we can see how in the course of our descent we have accumulated inheritances from the angelic plane as well as from our parents: there are characteristics that have accrued to us in the course of the descent that are not really us.

So far, we have been identifying with our inheritance and saying that we are the whole past that continues to live. That is what is seen from the worm's-eye view. From the eagle's-eye view, it is the other way around: we see that the inheritance that we have acquired from our parents is something that has accrued to us in the course of time, and that what we really are has had to accommodate itself to what we have inherited from our ancestors. What we really are is much more essential: it is what we have always been and will always be. It is the way the divine perfection manifests each time in a unique way; in a sense, it is as perfect as one could imagine. But it is perfect in its potentiality, not in its actuality; to be actuated, it must fecundate the qualities we inherit from our ancestors. Nevertheless, there are moments when we are really conscious of being what we really are, and those are the great moments in life. We suddenly experience ourselves as a being of light, or a being of joy. We may have suffered much, but we see that our being is really joy. Or we may see ourselves as a being of such light that it thrusts its light upon all things, or that we are really intelligence, sorting out all things and seeing all things. Or we can see that our real being is really nobility.

Occasionally, at the end of a meditation camp run by the Sufi Order, when people have reached a fairly high state, we do an exercise in which everyone would face another person and describe which of seven very high qualities they saw in that person. It is a form of positive darshan. A person might say, "I see a lot of light in you," or, "I see a lot of joy in you," or, "I see a lot of peace in you," or "I see a lot of wisdom in you," or, "I see a lot of power in you," or, "I see a lot of nobility in you"—whichever of the qualities we choose that they see. Interestingly, we find that there is a consensus as to what people see in one another; the majority of things they say concur with what other people say. It turns out to be a wonderful game of self-discovery, because sometimes what other people say confirms something we secretly feel in ourselves but we do not like adulation and do not want to assume anything. There is a kind of false humility in people who do not accept the grace of their beauty, and, of course, adulation is not always sincere, so it does not always ring true. But it is important for people to realize the glory of their being. It is often the case that people are continually degrading one and that life is constantly wearing down one's self–esteem and self–respect; there is a tendency to lose a sense of what one has always been. But if someone can convince us of what we really are, that is the ultimate therapy.

This is what real gurus are supposed to do: to grasp what a person is in his eternal being and turn a blind eye to what he has manifested, or actuated, in life. What most people see in another person is what has been actuated of the reality of the person in everyday life—what is called the personality. But if we refuse to see that—which is the secret of love, to turn a blind eye to the defects of a person—we can help a person to become what he really is. In the same way, when we teach healing we say that if you want to heal a person, you must imagine him well; you must never think of him as ill. So we can help a person to be convinced of what he is against his fear of being what he fears he might be, which is his personality. In fact, we can make him aware of his divine inheritance.

This is bringing a spiritual dimension into therapy. Some of these methods might be difficult to practice in a consulting room in conventional psychotherapy, and would be more successful in group therapy—for example, a version of the Cosmic Celebration or telling people about the divine qualities they manifest. One could also expose people to things they have always valued and have lost sight of, as in music and art therapy, or one could use walks as a method of getting in touch with the true self. Some of the methods of Murshid Samuel Lewis were extremely practical for bringing spirituality into everyday life, especially in walking —doing the walk of Buddha, the walk of Abraham, or the walk of Jesus. It is amazing how enacting a part can make us discover the being we are enacting in ourselves. There is the Buddha in our being, the Abraham in our being, and the Christ in our being: archetypes that are real in our beings. Buddha is very present in us. We inherit all these beings, because we inherit all beings whether incarnated or not; and we can discover them by enacting them. This is the secret of drama, which, unfortunately, has degenerated into psychodrama, which is getting into the unconscious instead of the superconscious. What we are talking about here is the superconscious. People who have participated in the Cosmic Celebration have sometimes been totally transformed for the rest of their lives. They were never the same afterwards, because they had suddenly discovered an aspect of their being that they had never known was there.

We are all actors on the stage of life, and we are playing roles, more or less, that are not as real as we think. Some of these are defense mechanisms: if we are afraid, sometimes we act as if we were not afraid, and if we dislike someone we act as if we liked him. There is a kind of insincerity in our role-playing. Perhaps we pretend to be efficient when we know we are not very efficient in our jobs. It's a masquerade—so why not play roles that we really are, even if we do not believe that we are them until we can discover them in ourselves? This is another form of therapy that can be carried out more in social interaction than in the consulting room.

The ultimate practice along these lines, which can be done both collectively and alone, is to get into the consciousness of the masters, saints, and prophets of all times. In discussing the development of certain qualities, we have noted that we can discover in ourselves the power that moves the universe, and the same intelligence that is working through all beings, looking, understanding, penetrating the secret of all things, and participating in the thinking behind the universe. But I have also said that one can only find oneself in another oneself. To make this more concrete, let us imagine that we have been pondering upon what is the quality that our life at present requires us to develop most, and we find that it is power. We find that we are lacking in power. But we cannot just strengthen our power, because that would be a terrible ego trip; we must somehow find a way of letting the power beyond our own power come through until we are able to identify with this divine power. If we were to concentrate on the being of Abraham, that would be a much more tangible way of proceeding than simply thinking about divine power. Divine power is so vague that it is beyond our grasp, but Abraham is, for us, a prototype of the father archetype, or authority and strength. We can find Abraham in our being, as I have said, and we can do this by identifying with Abraham rather than thinking about him. Imagining what it is like to be Abraham frees us from our identification with our self-image and enables us to develop the power of Abraham by getting into his consciousness. I can testify from personal experience that if I am able to meditate, it is because of having gotten into the consciousness of great beings upon whom I have meditated.

At a meditation camp once, a man once approached me and said, "Pir Vilayat, we try to follow your instructions about meditation, but it just doesn't seem to work as well as when you meditate with us." I found this flattering to my ego, but I said, "No, that's not the way I work. I want to give you the means of doing it without your having to depend on me, and that is why I'm giving you the instructions." I was very proud of my answer, because I felt that a guru really is supposed to make his pupils independent of himself. But then I spent a very bad night, and the next day I said, "You know, if I am able to meditate, it is because I have been meditating with such high beings, and somehow all that I have to do is get into the consciousness of those beings, and then I can meditate. But if I were to follow the very same instructions that I give, I wouldn't be able to meditate myself." This was a terrible admission to have to make, but it is that the only way in which I can hope to be helpful at all is if I am able to communicate something of the attunement I get from those beings rather than only the words. We must work on several planes at the same time: in teaching meditation, I am explaining things at the mind level, and at the same time something is working at other levels. And that is, in fact, the only way to practice psycho-therapy.

Chapter 12:

WORKING WITH ENERGY

We now come to methods that involve working with energy, working with sound, and working with light, among other elements. When I described the meditation in which we watch the body and say that it is not *our* body but only a lump of flesh made up of the fabric of the planet, there may have been an element of contempt implied in that meditation: "I couldn't possibly be my liver, or my heart, or whatever." But when we really start looking into the body, we realize that it is a universe of marvels. We might call it crystallized intelligence: the way the cells replicate and take in food from the environment—the way proteins are broken down by the pancreas and the gastrointestinal tract, pummeled by the enzymes, classified by the liver, and finally introduced through the membranes of the cells—these processes are evidence of an extraordinary intelligence in the body. The whole machinery of the body—the way the enzymes of the neurons of the brain give a briefing to the cells and the way all the functions of the body are connected by the very delicate balance of the autonomic nervous system, the secretion of hormones, and the neurotransmitters—is incredibly devised. It seems to be hierarchical: the cells are endowed with a degree of intelligence, picking up information, learning, and passing that information on to their progeny. It is as if there were many beings within our being.

The molecules within the cells are structured by the controlling devices of the genetic code, and are enabled to change the patterns and to radiate magnetism and light, and to vibrate at various pitches. If we could hear the music of the body, see the light that is emanated from it, and enter into the intelligence of the cells, we would never speak about our bodies contemptuously; we would be full of respect and admiration for the marvel that is placed at our disposal. When I say, "at our disposal," it sounds as though the body were something other than ourselves, but this is just a habit of thought; the beauty lies in the fact that we are part of the transience of the cells and the molecules, the mind, and the personality, and yet also somehow transcend all that is transitory in us by the passage from matter to spirit and spirit to matter.

The body is a very gently poised mechanism that is continually responding to the environment; it has its own built-in feedback system, and it is subjected to a tremendous amount of stress. The mind complex added to the body is still more precarious; it can hardly be surprising that people develop illnesses. There have been studies of the influence of different emotions on the secretions of different endocrine glands that control parts of the autonomic nervous system and also the extent to which cells are able to take in nourishment. Under emotional stress, something has to give: some people develop schizophrenia, some people develop ulcers, and others have heart attacks. Cancer is often found among people who cannot speak about their emotional stress and perhaps even deny it to themselves; part of their therapy would be to get them to admit to someone what it is that is eating into their hearts. Perhaps they could be persuaded to speak at least to a tree, because they must express themselves. Another factor in the development of cancer can be the problem of being jammed in a situation; sometimes, out of kindness, a person can allow himself to be imprisoned in a situation until an illness develops, and in that case it may be necessary for him simply to change his environment, whether internally or externally, in order to get out of that feeling of being enclosed. There are so many new methods in the cure of cancer that it seems entirely possible that it will be eradicated within the next decade. But in the meantime, there are a number of things we can do.

Some of the ancient methods of India are based upon the use of energy, called *shaktipat*. It is not uncommon for some people who come into contact with a guru to be so overwhelmed by the energy of the guru that they fall to the ground in a fit. I do not advocate this method myself; it is very dangerous to overcharge a person's circuits in that manner, because it induces a state that is rather similar to a hypnotic state. But there are ways of working with energy that are very useful and that we can consider implementing.

We have all had moments when we felt very magnetic, and other moments when we felt as if we had no magnetism —as if we were absolutely sapped of our magnetism. It is possible even to be in a very good state of health but be without magnetism, or even to be in a poor state of health and yet have an enormous amount of magnetism, so this feeling is not connected necessarily with our physical health. I have met a rishi in India whose body was a wreck—he was well into his eighties—but who was exuding magnetism. The body emanates a magnetic field, part of which is electrostatic and part of which is electromagnetic—what has sometimes been called the "life field." There has been an increasing amount of work done in laboratories in this area, and it has been found that the acupuncture lines fall along nodes within that field. The field seems to be caused by the ionization of the cells of the body.

In working with energy, we learn to burn the fuel in our bodies more intensely to increase the strength of our magnetism. This results either in raising the temperature of the body or in increasing the amount of energy emanated by the body so that the magnetic field increases. There are rishis in India who live in the mountains and do not use much energy for physical work; some of them keep the temperature of their bodies a half a degree or a degree lower than the usual temperature of the body to adapt themselves to the cold. They have an enormous amount of energy, and not just from whatever food they eat, because some of them eat very little. There are many other sources of energy than just physical energy.

In India, there is a story about Prince Puran who was wrongly accused by his father and banished from his kingdom. Years later, he returned to the garden of the palace as a sannyasin, and as soon as he sat there, the whole garden began to flourish. That is the epitome of what we want to do: we want to be sources of life, so that wherever we go things will flourish. Some people have that ability; others find that wherever they go, everything breaks down. How can we be in the category of those who make things happen? We can do this by working with energy just as an artist works with clay or a musician with sound.

One of the principles of yoga is that in some ways we can consciously do things better that are normally done by the unconscious, while, at the same time, in some ways the unconscious does things better than the conscious mind. We can sometimes take a function that is autonomous and make it conscious, and then push it back into the unconscious again. This is exactly what happens in learning to play the piano: the student trains his hands to make the right motions until it becomes automatic. If he makes a mistake, he brings his playing back into his conscious mind again, makes the correct motions consciously, and then thrusts the process back into the unconscious. The unconscious mind can do certain things much better than the conscious mind. I knew a genius mathematician who was able to tell what any number would be multiplied to an extraordinarily high number of powers. When his friends asked him how he did it, he said, "It's yoga!" He let his unconscious mind do the work; if he had tried to do it consciously, he would never have been able to.

The body monitors its functions unconsciously, but if we can monitor them with our conscious mind, we can improve them. In discussing biofeedback, we noted that the conscious will was unable to affect directly autonomic functions, but that we were able to get a handle on them by means of visualizations and that it is possible to bring a greater will than our own into the system. That is the art of yoga and the secret of Sufism. How we can do this is difficult to describe; what we need to do is get into a feeling of harmony—to be totally in step with the harmony of the universe. Then the energy that is manifested in that harmony comes through us and controls the whole functioning of the cells of the body. We become totally integrated. We like to say that we get our will or our consciousness out of the way, but in fact what we do is get our will and our consciousness into sync with the whole harmony of the universe.

There is no doubt that the functions of the cell—the frequencies of the pulsations of the atoms and of the whole cell, the number of photons radiated by the cell, and the ionization or potential of the electromagnetic field—are connected with thought. That is the marvel of life: the interconnection and intermeshing between mind and body. It is as if there were a hotline between the enzymes of the brain and the enzymes of the cell that bypasses the whole autonomic nervous system, so that it is possible to have control of the entire body, right down into the cell.

The secret is in visualization, which is calling upon the creativity that is our true being, our highest gift. If we imagine that we are sitting in the presence of a master who is radiating a lot of magnetism, we begin to radiate magnetism —which means we are actually doing something to the body. *Kundalini* is the art of what is called in physiology "kindling," which is enhancing the energy in the different cells of the body simply by concentrating on them. If we concentrate very intensely on the plexus at the bottom of the spine, for example, we find that it does indeed begin to pulse. This is not imagination; we are actually doing something to that plexus. In the same way, to lift our arm, all we need do is think of our arm being lifted, and we lift it. By concentrating on the bottom of the spine, we enhance the energy in that center.

This practice is called releasing pent-up energy—kundalini, or the snake, as it is called. Every part of the body— every cell of the body—is like the cell in a battery; it is able to store energy, which can be released by the action of the mind. That is how we lift our arms: by releasing energy. And because the plexi of the autonomic system are all connected, the energy is relayed; by triggering off energy in one center, we trigger off energy in another. Normally, energy is triggered off from the brain down through the whole body; here we are doing the opposite—starting at the bottom of the spine and moving upwards. This, of course, is the danger of kundalini—that one is reversing the normal course of energy. I find it better to bring energy down into the body from what I call the celestial spheres rather than moving energy up from the bottom of the body—or, in any case, at least balancing the two. The nerve impulses can be overstressed by kindling; as a matter of fact, it can trigger off epilepsy, which is a form of kindling similar to backfiring in a car. That is why it is not uncommon to hear of people who have become victims of a kundalini technique that they trusted because it has been used for so long in the East: the way in which kundalini is taught varies from one school to another, and it is not often well controlled.

There are many bizarre phenomena that can be triggered off in the body by using control systems wrongly; we often hear of people crying out or jumping up like a frog or even levitating. This is supposed to be what they call *siddhis,* or developing powers, although there does not seem to be much point in it. I know yogis in India who stand on one foot for five years just to show they can stand on one foot —but it is most difficult to see the point of it. What we would like to do is connect the use of energy with healing, for example, or fulfilling our purpose in life.

We often find that a successful lawyer has a great deal of charisma, which is really magnetism, while the man who may know the case better loses because he has less magnetism. I am not speaking here of physical magnetism. We are endowed with magnetism at all levels: the level of the mind, the level of the personality, the level of the heart (a person with a great deal of magnetism of heart can touch the hearts of others,) the level of the soul (which is deeper than the emotion of the heart) and the level of the spirit (which is very rare and like champagne, bubbling over with a very fine energy). What I am suggesting is working with the magnetism of the spirit, if we do not want to be too "spaced out," and feel we must have our feet on the earth, then we can at least combine the level of the spirit with the other levels.

If we are working with the electromagnetic field or the

electrostatic field, which is the ground or base of the whole energy system of the body, the best way to go about it is consciously to establish a relationship between the magnetic field of the body and the magnetic field of the environment. The planet Earth has a magnetic field that is of exactly the same nature as our own magnetic field—an electromagnetic field that includes an electrostatic component. This is where the role of the mind over the body becomes clearer: when we expand consciousness, as we do in the cosmic meditation, then when we exhale we can be conscious of the flow of our own magnetic field into the magnetic field of the environment, and as we inhale we can do the opposite— draw the magnetic field of the environment into our own magnetic field. What we are doing, in fact, is using the energy of the electromagnetic field to shoot the electrons in our bodies a little farther away from the nucleus. If the atom is subjected to light, heat, or any other form of energy, it will get into an excited state, which means that the electrons will not remain in their shell at a certain distance from the protons but will start moving farther away. The more energy is introduced, the farther they will circulate. Ultimately they circulate not only in more distant shells around the atom, but, in some cases, they will circulate inside the molecule. That is what happens in an electric current: the ions are circulating not only in the molecule but in the entire length of the wire.

The body can be in exactly the same kind of excited state —a highly-ionized state in which it is charged with energy. The hands of a healer will cause a mist to form in an alcohol bubble chamber or even change the conformation of proteins. And there are certain thoughts that enhance energy and bring it right down into the body. Ecstasy is the wine of the holy sacrament that will bring the body into a highly-charged state. Most people are suffering from being low-key, and then the body begins to complain and kick up a fuss—we get illnesses. It has, in fact, been ascertained that very often people who fight cancer are the ones who are cured; the ones who give in are more likely to succumb. There is an attitude of the mind involved.

But there is no point in exuding energy unless it is helpful. The problem with the victims of kundalini is that they have an enormous amount of energy and do not know what to do with it, so they start rolling on the ground. We can, instead, use this energy for healing or for being a source of energy in the same way as Prince Puran, who made everything flourish around him. Then our energy will grow, because we are using it.

Curiously enough, electromagnetic energy can be wasted in heat, and that process is a form of entropy. There are some people who, when they are overenthused, develop a fever; many people get hot flashes when something very traumatic is happening, or even if they think of something that is very distressing. In that case, their energy is dissipated in heat. But the same energy that is dissipated in heat can be transposed into light, because that involves simply a question of frequency. Light is a higher frequency of the electromagnetic radiation. And among all the practices of meditation I know, the practices with light are the most inspiring and the most exciting. If I were to choose a path—and there are many different spiritual paths—I would choose the path of illumination. I feel that many other people feel the same way; if we tried to imagine a perfect being whom we would like as a guru, most of us would probably try to imagine someone who was totally luminous and radiant. But the fact is that we can be that ourselves; we need not project it onto another person.

The first thing to do in working with light is to enhance energy by ecstasy. My little niece was screaming her head off once, and when we asked what was wrong, she said, "I'm suffering from an overdose of ecstasy." What we have to do is take on an overdose of ecstasy and then do something with it instead of screaming or radiating heat: we have to transmute that energy into light. This is the only kind of kundalini work that I could subscribe to—transmuting energy into light. We do this by imagining the color red at the bottom of the spine; the color yellow in the heart center; the color blue in the eyes; the color violet in the third eye; and a diamond-like hue filled with all the colors of the spectrum in the crown center.

This process works because of the impact of thought on the radiation of the cells of the body. The cells are continually radiating photons, which means that the electrons are being transformed into photons, just as in a lamp. This phenomenon is called bioluminescence. The amount of light that is sent out by the cells varies, and it can be monitored by our thoughts. The secret is in the frequency; at the level of a very high frequency, we send out light in the violet or ultra–violet range; the middle-range frequencies are yellow or golden, in the heart; and we can also radiate infrared, which we feel in the heart of the body.

Ten years ago, people might have thought it was impossible that one could become more radiant by meditating on light; they would have considered it a hallucination. Now we know that the body does radiate light; it is not just sheer imagination. Actually, there is nothing more real than imagination, but we are living in a time when it is nice to be able to substantiate things. I have seen people come out of a retreat absolutely radiant. That is an observable fact and a repeatable fact; anyone can do it. If one could spare a week, it would be well worth that week to spend it meditating on light.

This form of energy is not reduced to the radiation of the body, although that is one of its components. There are other components that are more difficult to prove scientifically because they are beyond the frontier of what we call matter. The ancients called it the "uncreated light." The connection between the uncreated light and the created light is very difficult to describe. We are on shaky ground here from the point of view of those who are convinced that the only real things are those that can be ascertained by science, although, as I have already said, the physical world is just what emerges out of a universe that is far richer than whatever can come through at the physical level. Once we accept this, we can go on.

Concentrating on the crown center helps us to identify ourselves with another type of light than the light of the aura. How and why it works we do not know, but the different plexi of the autonomic nervous system, such as the heart chakra or the solar plexus, control certain functions and, therefore, are concerned with the mind-body dichotomy. If we turn our eyeballs upwards, press the tongue against the palate, and reach upwards in our thought, we can feel the descent of the uncreated light through the crown center. It is important not to concentrate simply on the point above the head that is the crown center, however, because it can only put one into an astral state.

It is important here to make a distinction between what is experienced in a higher state of meditation and what is experienced in astral travel. In astral travel, one is transferring the center of one's being elsewhere in space, whereas in higher states of meditation one is not displacing one's center in space but is discovering a totally different space; in fact, there is no location in space at all. That is why there is some danger in trying to lift one's consciousness geographically, let us say above the head, and that is the point at which many people flounder: it is, again, the danger of kundalini, because one is transferring one's consciousness from the bottom of the spine upwards, and if one continues moving upwards, there is a sense of being located somewhere else higher up in space, which induces the astral state. The major problem with astral travel, or out–of–body experience, is that one tends to make a loose connection between the body and that level, and the consequence is that one can never reach higher because one has hit a ceiling there; one cannot go higher—and by "higher" I do not mean geographically, but spiritually.

The juncture that gives us access to the uncreated light has to do with our thinking; it is thinking of the source from which we derive our light. We think of ourselves passively with regard to the divine action. We began by thinking actively to enhance the energy in our bodies and radiate light. Now we do the reverse and experience how we are able to channel a light that is not of our own making. The Sufis call it the "descending light" instead of the "ascending light"; in the Qur'an there is a saying about a light upon a light, and the early Christians also made a distinction between these two different kinds of light, the created light and the uncreated light.

Now, once more, we must avoid a pitfall that we find throughout meditation and that we have been coming across throughout this book. There are two ways of looking at experience: one is to say, "I am the eyes through which God sees," and the other is to say, "I am the divine glance"; one is to say, "I allow the divine power to come through me," and the other is to say, "I am the divine power"; one is to say, "I have been shattered by the descent of the holy spirit," and the other is to say, "I am pure spirit." There are two opposites, and throughout this book we have always encountered this reconciliation of the irreconcilables. I am always saying that we are both, even though this does not seem possible. We are both the part and the totality, both eternal and transient, both the eyes through which God sees and the divine glance. Our metaphysical assumptions stand in the way of our experience; when we can reach this holistic view, which says that everything is an unbroken wholeness and therefore no one of us can say that he is a part, from that moment onwards we have overcome a mental objection to our experience and the way is open to experiencing.

The breakthrough comes when we can say, "Now I know what I am; I am a being of light." It is one of the most important moments in our lives when we realize that all this time we thought we were a personality, a body, and so on —and, of course, we are that also, but now we really know what we are. This is borne out by memories of the unconscious of the sort that Jung wrote about—memories that come through in dreams. Our experience tallies with our memory of prenatal states. All this is, however, a futile effort to try to substantiate something that is given directly. We do not need to substantiate it. We either accept it or not. We have the experience, and it is either meaningful to us or it is not. The moment that it is meaningful is the one that makes all the difference.

That moment makes all the difference to our being. There is quite a difference between radiating light—the light of the aura—and experiencing oneself as a being of light, because, for one thing, the light of the aura is localized, centered in a certain location in space, and is a physical phenomenon, whereas being a being of light is a totally different nature of reality than the spatial-temporal one. This is why the Sufis always associate the term "being of light" with the term "luminous intelligence"; for the Sufis, intelligence is an un-created light. This is, perhaps, a metaphor—a way of saying that there comes a time when we are aware that wherever we go we throw light upon all things and that what we see is the way things react to that light, as they do to the light of the sun.

We not only send out light; we even do the opposite—draw light into the body in photosynthesis. The cells of our bodies are capable of photosynthesis, just like plants, and this is also a phenomenon of the aura. We can work with the aura not only to enhance our energy and transform heat energy into ultraviolet light, but also to draw light from the environment and radiate it out. This, too, involves the control of the will. Certain molecules are able to store light energy and release it in the form of photons.

In speaking of radiating the uncreated light, we are talking about something totally different: the penetration of a noëtic reality into physical reality. In fact, we can say that ultimately we are intelligence. There is a difference between consciousness and intelligence; Hazrat Inayat Khan describes it very clearly when he says that intelligence becomes consciousness when it is faced with an object. If we were to deprive our consciousness of an object—if, for example, we were in a sensory-deprivation tank—if we were not experiencing anything through our senses and were doing a type of meditation in which we emptied our mind of thought so that the mind was blank, what would happen to consciousness? It would be resorbed in its ground, which is intelligence. This is the *turiya* state of *advaya* yoga.

This is one of the practices that leads to samadhi, and samadhi is the secret of intuition. The practice of samadhi can give us access to experiencing ourselves as luminous intelligence, because samadhi is by definition a state in which we have stripped ourselves of all our identifications with the body, the mind, the emotions, the personality, and even consciousness. In the end, all that remains of our sense of identity is being pure intelligence, pure energy (or spirit), and pure ecstasy. That is what the samadhi state is: luminous intelligence, which is conceived of as light by the Sufis —the uncreated light.

If we are in a state of reverie, we can, instead of letting ourselves be overwhelmed by random thoughts, prefigure the meandering of the mind by feeding an input into it before getting into a state of reverie (which is a form of dream therapy), so that we will be able to muster memories of worlds of light—landscapes of light, beings of light, and ourselves as beings of light. All this can come back to us again, and it is the most inspiring thing that can happen to us. As a matter of fact, the dreams of illuminated beings become extremely beautiful, because they partake of the rediscovery of one's origin as a being of light.

Dream therapy is also one of the techniques that can be used in therapy with very good chances of success. People with epilepsy often have bad dreams, sometimes night-mares, and so some doctors have realized that there is some relationship between the visualizations of the dream world and the physical symptoms, and have wondered whether, since it is so difficult to deal with the physical symptoms, one could not deal with the psychological symptoms that have triggered off the physiological ones. Working with dreams is one way to do this, and it, too, is similar to a biofeedback system. Children like to have stories read to them before they go to sleep, and this is very important because it is a kind of dream therapy: by reading to them, we prepare them to rediscover the whole world inside them-selves. We cannot be sure of the effect of some of the televi-sion programs they are exposed to. For a long time, my own son used to dream of dragons rather than fairies. We should, no doubt, prepare our children for the hard world, but a few fairies here and there would be quite helpful, instead of only dragons.

We have encountered the difficulty of working with dreams in our discussion of the state of reverie. We cannot affect our thinking in any way in a state of reverie; in fact, that is what the state of reverie is about. We can affect it only prior to getting into it, by monitoring our thoughts. One of the techniques used in meditation is to delve into the world of light before one goes to sleep; one can do medita-tions on different colors or any of the innumerable images of light—landscapes of light, or whatever. There are many beautiful pictures that are like visitations of beings of light; we might want to go back to our children's storybooks, some of which can be really inspiring and can be better appreciated by grown-ups than by children. They were written by grown-ups, anyway. Then, when we sleep, we will continue dreaming about what we have read about.

There are many stories among the Sufis about their visions of heavenly spheres, like the visions of Avicenna or Suhrawardhi. Shihab ad-din Suhrawardhi is one of the most wonderful examples of a mystic who probes into the worlds of light, and he said he was inspired by the tradition of the Zoroastrian Magi and that he had recovered some of the secrets of Persepolis. The library at Persepolis is said to have been destroyed by the troops of Alexander the Great, but Suhrawardhi said that in higher planes, he rediscovered some of the secrets of the Magi. One of these was a method of attuning oneself to the consciousness of cosmic beings; the planets, for instance, are always seen as the embodiments of beings. Nowadays, most people do not think in these terms; they think of the planets as being just lumps of minerals. For the Sufis, all is life. There is an archangel of the planet Earth and an archangel of the sun, and Prince Hurakhsh who, according to the Sufis, is a true being of light —a radiant being. Our bodies may be fractions of the planet, but our souls are a fraction of the being of the archangel of light of the planet Earth, who is in turn part of the archangel of light of the sun, and so on. There is a hierarchy of beings of light that we perceive in a "felt thought" of being derived light from a being who is hierarchically superior to us in the realms of light. So we are transmitting a heavenly light upon the earth.

These things may sound rather extravagant, but we are touching upon something that is very important in releasing the human being from the despair of identifying with matter. That identification weighs very heavily upon people. The real redemption is to be released from it, and it is all in the mind—all a question of how one looks at things. It is as if we were to show a child a puzzle in which there are some trees and ask him, "Can you see the little birdie in the tree?" "No, I can't see the birdie." "Look again. Can you see it?" "Yes!" That is a moment of breakthrough: the child is able to see something he had not seen before. That is what therapy is all about: seeing something we had not seen before. That is also the secret of evolution: what makes the human being human is his ability to see relationships that other animals cannot see. Now we are speaking about seeing things that require a very subtle ability—and it is the vision of the human being that makes the greatness of the human being.

There is a practice that we use in the Sufi Order that is called the "dhikr of light." It consists in surveying the aura with light as if one were a searchlight that is casting its beam upon the aura, in a circular motion from left to right; then one reverses the orientation of one's consciousness and turns it upwards towards the light of which one is the expression. Then one reverses things again and experiences oneself as being the light that one is supposed to channel—because we are both the eyes through which God sees and also the divine glance. One transposes one's consciousness into the *nur al-anwar*—the "light upon the light"—that is the source of all light, and illuminates one's aura with the light of the heavens.

The beauty of this is that if we just worked with the aura we might become rather conceited. In the hermetic tradition the light of the aura has been called, quite rightly, Luciferian light; it is light that has become disconnected from its source. That is why it is so important to re-establish our connection with the source of light. And, in fact, that is the secret of the Magi: reconnecting with the source of light, which the Zoroastrians call *xvarnah,* the crown of the king. We must reestablish our connection with the source of light and look upon ourselves passively with regard to it, as a ray of that light but also as that light itself, because there is no distinction between the rays of the sun and the sun itself.

We began by working with magnetism and discussed working at both ends—I said that it was permissible to work with earth energy as long as we also work with spirit. There are several modes of energy, such as electromagnetic and gravitational energy; there is also psychic energy, and there is the energy of pure spirit. It is the energy of pure spirit that is the catalyst, and it is something one experiences at rare moments. I described the state in which we feel we need to get into the mountains and get in contact with the snow and the ice, away from the lush vegetation and the sham of the world. That is a state of the soul—a kind of attunement, the attunement of the pilgrim who is always pictured climbing the mountain. In order to climb that mountain, we find that we have to strip off many things that we thought we needed, until we are finally laid bare and experience ourselves as pure spirit. This is the immaculate state, embodied in the Virgin Mary.

The process that strips us is a search for truth, for authenticity. This is why we gradually let go of things we had clad ourselves with in order to "make it" in the rat race. The image of snow is appropriate when we have a need for truth, simplicity, and purity, because we feel as if we have to take off our shoes so that we will not pollute the snow with the mud on our shoes, and we feel like purifying our thoughts and emotions so that they are perfectly immaculate, so that we may be allowed to enter into this landscape of the soul. It is as if we were on a quest for the source of life, which we sometimes represent as a fountainhead in the high mountains; the main idea is to get away, as a pilgrim, from all we have gotten mixed up with, so that we can discover ourselves as pure spirit. It may be that on the way back we experience ourselves as touched upon by the spirit; this is one of the experiences of the high mystics. In this experience, we may still be in our personal consciousness. But at a certain point we reach the realization that we are pure spirit.

There is no energy that is more overwhelming and more effective than this. In fact, it is the one that triggers off all the other forms of energy. It is a shortcut that can replace trying to work with magnetism or even with light; if we are able to touch upon this form of energy, then all the other forms will be triggered off. It is the secret of healing. That is why Christ told his disciples, "Go and heal with the spirit." And they were able to do it in spite of their own disbelief at first. It is unusual to meet a being who is pure spirit, but one guru we met in India was just that: bubbling over with pure spirit, the highest form of energy. He filled the room with that energy, and we were all just lifted beyond ourselves by the energy of the spirit.

This kind of energy is not to be encountered simply by turning our eyes upward, pressing upward with the tongue, and moving the consciousness; it comes from the attitude of being void and by "preparing the temple." By cleaning the temple, we eventually arrive at a point of voidness, called *sunyata* in Buddhism; we become immaculate. One image we could represent to ourselves is a crystal, because there is a certain kind of void in a crystal. The spaces between the molecules are such that the light is able to pass through the voidness. When we arrive at a state that is similar to that of the crystal, we realize that we are pure spirit. It is the opposite of kundalini: we can work with this energy downwards and can use it for healing. And we can use it to change the situations in our lives totally.

MEDITATIONS WITH ENERGY

Relax the muscles of your back: the bottom of your back, the bottom of the spine, the middle of the back, the shoulder blades, the shoulders; relax the jaw and the inside of the skull.

Exhale very deeply and inhale without effort. Then exhale still longer and inhale without effort.

Scatter your consciousness into the vastness as you exhale and experience yourself as a convergence of the universe as you inhale. Then think of your body as dust that is scattered in space as you exhale, and think of it as being coagulated as you inhale. Let your thoughts be scattered or "spaced out" as you exhale, and then reformed as you inhale. Let your personality be dismantled as you exhale, and let the forces of nature build it up anew in a rebirth as you inhale.

Once more, extend consciousness as you exhale. This time, you get into the divine consciousness; you merge into the divine consciousness of the total universe, and then as you inhale you experience your consciousness as an eddy, or vortex, or whirlpool that has formed itself in the ocean of consciousness. Then you go back into the ocean again.

EARTH ENERGY

We want to work with energy, to dynamize ourselves with fresh energy; and we want to go through an absolutely total purification at all levels of our being, becoming re-freshed, renewed, and regenerated. So first of all, we have to re-establish our contact with Mother Earth. Concentrate on the energy that arises from the earth in the bottom of your spinal cord (the *muladhara chakra*), and then you can drain out polluted magnetism into the earth. You will have to feel the electromagnetic field around your body, particularly around your arms, like a zone of charged particles around your body.

As you exhale, you must feel how this zone, or area, or etheric body, or whatever you may wish to call it, is drawn into the earth, downwards, and drained from your body; and the essential point of contact is, of course, the muladhara center at the bottom of the spine. As you inhale, you should be aware of the magnetism of the earth. It is very slight: it is not a very powerful force. It is the force that is used by mariners when they use a compass to steer their course.

You could concentrate on both the chakra at the bottom of the spine and also the chakras in the hands, so as you inhale you are drawing this energy from the earth. While you are radiating energy out through your hands, you let the polluted magnetism of your body be drained through the muladhara chakra back into the earth field. By this time you should feel a very high intensity field of magnetism around your body, which also permeates the cells of the body, continually drawing fresh energy from the magnetic field of the earth and draining itself back into the magnetic field of the earth. It is your your contact with Mother Earth—your covenant with Mother Earth.

ENERGY OF THE SPIRIT

Now, having worked with earth energy, we shall work with celestial energy. In its highest form, this is the energy of the holy spirit. It is associated with the crown center.

As you inhale, you must turn your eyeballs upwards and press your tongue against the palate. Attune your whole being to this very fine, very subtle form of energy. Just imagine walking in a landscape of ice and snow; and you need not only to be wary of cleaning the mud off your shoes because you don't want to pollute the snow, you must also strip yourself of most of yourself, so that only the very finest, gossamer quintessence of your being is able to reach into these spheres. It is as if you were jettisoning ballast from a balloon so that you are able to rise higher.

Now you have to concentrate on the aperture at the top of the head. Imagine that the crown center is as the yogis describe it—a million-petalled lotus—and it opens up. The whole lotus opens up under the action of the rising magnetism of the earth that is triggered off by your thoughts, your concentration. This allows that very subtle quintessence of your being to rise.

This is just a model, because in fact, you are not being displaced in space. There is only a switch in the focus of consciousness into higher levels of the universe, or into universes other than the physical one. There is no displacement in space: I am saying this so that you can avoid doing astral projection. What you are doing is becoming conscious of something that is, and that is all here; at least, it is not somewhere else in space. In fact, it is not in space at all, as we understand it.

You have an image of landscapes of snow and ice, just in order to make you feel intensely purified and very peaceful, to the point that you enjoy the cold. In fact, you open the pores of your body to the cold and let all that energy seep right into the pores of your skin, and then deep into the bones, so that you are just part of the immaculate scene. You are a pilgrim in the high Himalayas—stripped bare, purified, free, immaculate, disintoxicated, anesthetized, depersonalized—in search of the waters of life, which is pure energy, or, rather, the life of life, the catalyst that triggers off the latent energy in all things: pure spirit. And you have to touch upon it; you have to reach that part of yourself that is spirit and reestablish the connection.

Just think of yourself as being pure spirit. You have arrived at such a fine state of stripping that you are just spirit. And the only way to reconcile the thought of any denseness of the body is to think of the body as different layers that you have incorporated in the course of your descent. Now you are reversing the course of descent, so think of the layers as being just formations with which you have established some kind of connection; but the quintessence of your being is pure spirit.

As you exhale, you experience your descent: the descent of spirit. This is not the same as imagining that *you* are being quickened by the spirit, because then you would be identifying yourself with the transient layers of your being. As you rise, you discover; to discover means you uncover, and finally you realize your real identity. It is all in the mind: it is all a matter of realization. You rid yourself of your opinion about what you are, and discover another way of looking upon yourself, which is more reliable because it is unchanging. All the things you thought you were are changing and are, therefore, formations. Now as you exhale, and while you experience yourself as descending, you have a feeling of quickening the flesh with what you are, which is pure spirit. You are catalyzing its setting, triggering off latent energy, vivifying every cell of the body. That is the last stage at the end of the exhalation. On the way down, there is a descent through all the different bodies: the body of light, the mind, and the etheric and astral bodies—all the different bodies are dynamized.

The consequence is that the cells begin to dance. That is one of the meanings of the "dance of Shiva." Everything springs to life under the action of spirit: it is like awakening the sleeping princess. The rays of the sun awaken the little shoots that are frozen through the night and are now drinking the dew; all things spring to life.

It is very useful to become aware of the cells of the body, of all the activity that is going on in them: mitosis, the proliferation of the cells, the flow of blood through the cells, the ionic flow of magnetism through the cells, and the activity of the cells metamorphosing the environment, which is the food, into their own material (what is called replication). You can experience all these phenomena, and you can experience how the whole process is triggered off by the magic wand of spirit. It is a kind of magic, how all this takes place.

Now, every time you inhale and turn your eyeballs upward, the lotus opens up at the top of your head and you strip—you become pure spirit. And every time you exhale, you infuse all the different bodies, including the physical body, with pure spirit. At that time the whole process of life is spurred, intensified, enhanced, dynamized.

Now you can combine the two poles of your being—the bottom of the spine and the top of the head. As you are drawing earth energy through the bottom of the spine, your consciousness is free to rise in the crown center, above the crown center, and go through the immaculate state, while your body is being dynamized by the earth. Then, as you exhale, you can concentrate on being pure spirit infusing the body, while all the polluted magnetism is being drained through the bottom of the spinal cord, the muladhara chakra.

You could also think of the linkage of the magnetism of the earth and the magnetism of the heavens. You could pull energy in at both ends at the same time as you inhale, and you would find that these two forms of energy—celestial energy and earth energy—mingle just like hot and cold water in the faucet in the solar plexus.

PRANA ENERGY

What I would advise doing now is incorporating a third form of energy, the energy of prana, which also flows into the solar plexus, so that you have three sources of energy, or three portals or inlets through which energy is drawn into the body. Prana energy is neither earth energy nor celestial energy. You could, perhaps call it energy from outer space. Scientifically, it is gravitational energy, which is a much greater power than electromagnetic energy. It is like the deformation of space through its condensation due to matter; the presence of matter will always deform space or cause stress upon space's landscape. Your body, for example, is like a dry patch in an orange, which draws the rest of the orange into itself: it stresses the orange. In that sense, that point of stress is linked with the whole rest of the universe, so you are able to draw that power of the universe into yourself by your sense of yourself, which is the ego.

Then you can do the opposite: when you lose the sense of your ego, then you reach out into the vastness of space. There is even a change in the cells of the body that are not under stress anymore—in the proteins. There is a deconformation of the cells. There is something that happens to the cells that get into a different phase as your consciousness scatters in the universe: they change again. There is a conformation pattern that takes place in the nerves as you inhale—as you become aware of your ego—and at that moment, as you inhale, you are drawing energy from outer space. It is best to think of yourself as a vortex—a whirlpool. Forces are set up in a whirlpool; the energy of the whole lake, or ocean, is converged in the whirlpool. And, in a sense, that is something that happens to your consciousness: by thinking of yourself as being a point of convergence in the whole universe, you unleash the forces of the universe in

154

yourself. You allow the forces of the universe in yourself to build up, and you experience the whole universe converging in you—the whole ocean heaving up in one wave.

COMBINING EARTH, SPIRIT, AND PRANA ENERGY

Now you can combine all three forms of energy at the same time as you inhale: you can inhale through the bottom of the spine, the top of the head, and the solar plexus, drawing in all those three forms of energy. But a far better way of putting it is to say that you *are* each of those forms of energy. You are not just the magnetism of the earth, which is really the transmutation of mass into energy; you are the power of the whole universe. As you exhale, you not only reach out into the vastness; your consciousness reaches beyond space—not in any direction of space, but beyond any spatial extension—and also deep into the earth.

LIGHT ENERGY

Now we can work with the transmutation of fire into light. As you exhale, you can enhance the burning process in your body by thinking of your body as being like hot coals; you are blowing upon those coals, and consequently they burn more brightly. You produce heat in your body, and you should feel a flush of heat around your body, like an infrared radiation, as you exhale. As you inhale, concentrate first of all on a golden color, like the sun, in your heart center, then blue in your eyes, violet in your third eye, and a diamond-like hue in the crown center, with all kinds of reflections of all the colors of the spectrum in it. Then, as you exhale, you experience not so much a hot infrared radiation anymore, but a radiation that has become much more light than fire; and it gives you a feeling of coolness rather than heat.

Now we shall have to halve the inhaling and the exhaling. In the first half of the inhaling, you are burning intensely, but are also drawing radiation from the atmosphere. In the second half of the inhaling, you concentrate on the higher chakras—the golden, blue, and violet light. In the first half of the exhaling, you are radiating light, the light of the aura, and in the second half, you are radiating heat and infrared radiation as you enhance the burning process in your body. Now, in the first half of the inhaling again, you draw radiation from outer space, and in the second half concentrate upon the higher chakras, enhancing their light rather than their heat. Then as you exhale, in the first half you are radiating light and the second half heat. As you inhale, you are drawing in radiation in the first half, and in the second half transmuting fire into light—transmuting light in the higher chakras. In the first half of the exhalation, radiate light again, and then continue in the cycle.

What we are learning to do is to work with energy and dynamize ourselves. And it is that energy that transmutes consciousness, or shifts consciousness from its very narrow purview into higher states of awareness leading to awakening—which is our ultimate goal.

Chapter 13:

THE ART OF PERSONALITY

In the architecture of my music I want to demonstrate to the world the architecture of a new and beautiful social commonwealth. The secret of my harmony? I alone know it. Each instrument in counterpoint, and as many contrapuntal parts as there are instruments. It is the enlightened self-discipline of the various parts, each voluntarily imposing on itself the limits of its individual freedom for the well-being of the community. That is my message. Not the autocracy of a single stubborn melody on the one hand, nor the anarchy of unchecked noise on the other. No, a delicate balance between the two; an enlightened freedom. The science of my art. The art of my science. The harmony of the stars in the heavens, the yearning for brotherhood in the heart of man. This is the secret of my music.

Johann Sebastian Bach

We have been discussing, and experiencing, things that run so close to the experience of the mentally disturbed that it seems quite reasonable that we might like to know how to tell the difference. It is far from my intention to make people more "spaced out" than they already are, and it should be clear that one must have a great deal of strength to handle these experiences. In most of the authentic schools in the East, there is a requirement that a pupil be in good mental health before making a retreat or engaging in transcendent experiences. The question is, where is the dividing line? How can we tell the difference between a genuine experience and a mental aberration?

We encountered a few guidelines in describing the difference between imagination and fantasy, when we found that the dividing line, if there is any, is between being in the mainstream and branching off into blind alleys. The whole cosmic imagination gathers itself together into the DNA of man instead of scattering itself in all kinds of side issues; there seems to be a very definite direction, even though it sometimes branches off here and there. The process is one of trial and error. In the same way, the imagination working through our minds is constructive when it is totally in sync, or in harmony, with the whole harmony of the universe. This is not something that is fixed; it is always growing. What concerns us is the degree of integration. My comparison of the nails and hair to the brain cells is not a perfect one, because the jagged ends—the nails and hair—contain the same DNA that is in the brain cells; perhaps the case of cancer cells is a clearer example of cells that have alienated themselves from the order, thus raising the question of whether they are or are not part of the body. In the same way, thoughts can get alienated from the order and become random.

There is, of course, an irrational element in the psyche, which cannot be dealt with by reasoning. This is a symptom of entropy—the disintegration of all composite things, be they matter or the psyche. In order to be rebuilt, things must break down, and if one clings to one's sense of identity, there is a fear of disintegration—and, what is more, there is randomness in this disintegration rather than programming.

There is a fear of being handed into a world that has gone mad, which is the experience of people in a concentration camp—the feeling that perhaps there is no program at all, and that all is random.

This touches upon the problem of faith and belief. In our time, we are rebelling against authority. This is a natural part of growth, and it is the means by which the organism on the whole overcomes sclerosis—the tendency to become static rather than dynamic. To progress, there must be some risk involved; and, in fact, it is the constituent elements of the totality that bring about the variations. The management of a firm may have its preconceived ideas about how to run things, but the people on the production line may also have their proposals for change; one of the reasons for the tremendous success of Japanese industry is its management organization, which takes into account the feedback from the people on the line. This is where rebellion has a part to play. The problem of authority has also been pointed up by Stanley Milgram's experiment in which volunteers administered electric "shocks" to "learners" in what had been represented to them as a teaching experiment. (In fact, the "learners" were actors and actresses and the "shocks" were nonexistent.) The extent to which people under the impact of authority were willing to cause actual physical damage to others to "teach" them turned out to be extraordinary.

Authority has its part to play in the scheme of things to maintain coherence in the parts of the whole, but rebellion has its role in keeping the organism in a dynamic state so that it progresses. There is a balance between those two, but whenever the forces of disintegration become overwhelming, as happens in a patient whose mind is breaking down, there is fear. Because it is an irrational fear, it may be interpreted in many different ways—as fear of the unknown, or fear of phantoms of the mind—and it can lead to seeking refuge in what seems to the therapist to be an unreal world. This leads to a further problem, which is the feeling of being trapped; as we have noted earlier, this feeling is one of the causes of schizophrenia, as well as of cancer. Something—either the mind or the body—has to give.

Some people who are mentally disturbed have difficulty in relating to other people because of the feeling that they themselves are really special. These are people who have lost their contact with the totality. Other people believe only in "What I can see and what I can touch," and so cut themselves off from the richness of the entire reality of the universe. Since our representation of the universe is important for our unfoldment, as long as we maintain a narrow personal vantage point our growth will be impeded by the limitation of our grasp of the universe as well as the limitation of our self-image. The only way, as the alchemists have shown, to bring about any progress at all is to go through a breakdown that will eventually aver itself to be a breakthrough, as R. D. Laing describes it. When this process of disintegration, which is entropy, gets out of hand, schizophrenia results; the great art of the therapist is to know how to stem the tide and reverse the process so that the patient can begin to rebuild his personality.

As we have noted, creativity is extremely important; most people suffer because life does not offer them the opportunity to be creative, and because they tend to distrust their creativity. Creativity has to do with the ability to grasp reality on its way down into actuality—what the Sufis call the unmanifested on its way down to the manifest. The human being has access to realms that are not irrational but super-rational. Those are the realms of the archetypes; as Shakespeare wrote, "As imagination bodies forth/ The forms of things unknown, the poet's pen/ Turns them into shapes, and gives to airy nothing/ A local habitation and a name." Infinity and eternity are archetypes; there is no such thing as infinite space, but infinity does exist as an archetype.

Most of our thoughts are reactions to the environment, which are not creative. Being creative is being able to give shape to what was originally cosmic emotion and cosmic understanding. One of the things we do in meditation is to reach into the programming of the universe. It is extraordinary to realize that our body should be part of the fabric of the planet—is, in fact, the proliferation of the planet—but it is still more extraordinary to realize that we have access to the programming behind the universe and are ourselves part of that programming. We are not puppets that have to toe the line. Unless our meditation is limited by preconceived ideas—which is something we must be most careful about—we can let our minds reach beyond themselves until we find ourselves able to grasp the programming. This is programming that is dynamic rather than static; it is continually reprogrammed.

Inventiveness, imagination, and creativity are always trial and error: the programming of the universe is tentative, not fixed. We might imagine a computer that is able to reprogram its software on the strength of the feedback it gets—and, what is more, is able to progress only by taking risks. The most interesting thing is the relationship between the wills of the parts and the total will, which is best described by Johann Sebastian Bach: "Each instrument in counterpoint, and as many contrapuntal parts as there are instruments . . . Not the autocracy of a single stubborn melody," as when there is a melody and an accompaniment. Every theme contributes towards the harmony of the whole, and every theme limits its prerogatives in the interest of the harmony of the whole. Bach goes on to say that this is "the harmony of the stars in the heavens." He knew what he was doing: "In the architecture of my music I want to demonstrate to the world the architecture of a new and beautiful social commonwealth." A commonwealth is a social organization in which each being participates freely in the well-being of the totality, but in which each being also restricts his freedom for the sake of the totality. Each person need not simply fit into the program; each contributes to the program organically.

The totality is invested in each part, and if a single part is unscrupulous, it can throw the entire scheme into disarray: it is entirely possible that one insane person, with enough money to build his own atomic bomb, could destroy the planet. That is the risk taken by God to make us free: every part can involve the totality.

Imagination incorporates the order of the universe—the dynamic, not the static order; in the works of Bach, we feel he is describing something of the order of the universe, which is continually finding new ways of performing better than it has done before. When we have access to the divine programming, we see that it is goal-oriented; it is always moving toward new horizons. So the most important thing we can do in psychotherapy is to encourage people to be creative—and to remember that the ultimate work of art is the personality. From the moment one realizes that there is nothing one cannot become if one really wishes it, one attains the ultimate optimism, which makes sense of one's life. The schizophrenic especially no longer wishes to toe the line, to enter into those categories that have been imposed by society. He has awakened from a certain vantage point, and has alienated himself from communication with other people because he feels they are caught up in a way of thinking that he himself has outgrown. But, having alienated himself, he has lost the very purpose of life, and is running amok in the realm of imagination. The whole importance of the imagination is that it should be concretized.

The practical mystic is able to make use of his or her experiences. The difference between the schizophrenic and the mystic is that the mystic is really creative. We might say that the difference is between going to fetch one's inspiration and making something out of it or just losing oneself in no man's land without any purpose. The person who is mentally ill has allowed himself to get lost. The mystic does something with the energy he or she encounters and makes an effort to concretize as much as possible that richness of experience that is almost too indefinable to make concrete. Saint Theresa of Avila was a very practical and active woman, yet her experiences were absolutely ineffable and out of time and space. That is the criterion of the mystic: to be able to cross the threshold and still find one's way back into the world of time and space, and bridge the two.